D0719663

Where Have All the Intellectuals Gone?

Also available from Continuum:

Culture of Fear (revised edition), Frank Furedi

Killing Thinking: Death of the University, Mary Evans

Mass Media in a Mass Society: Myth and Reality, Richard Hoggart

Where Have All the Intellectuals Gone?

Confronting 21st Century Philistinism

Frank Furedi

continuum
LONDON • NEW YORK

Continuum
The Tower Building
11 York Road
London SE1 7NX
www.continuumbooks.com

15 East 26th Street
New York
NY 10010

© Frank Furedi 2004

British Library Cataloguing-in-Publication Data
A catalogue record for this book is available from the British Library.

ISBN: 0-8264-6769-5 (hardback)

Typeset by BookEns Ltd, Royston, Herts.
Printed and bound in Great Britain

Contents

Preface

For some time now I have been disturbed by the profound sense of intellectual disorientation that appears to afflict many of our cultural institutions, universities and schools. The public deserves a high quality of intellectual debate from our cultural institutions and, as an audience with infinite potential, should command far greater respect. This book is written for the many intelligent men and women who aspire to a more challenging intellectual and cultural life.

The ideas presented in *Where Have All the Intellectuals Gone?* were developed through a protracted conversation with friends and colleagues. The steady stream of correspondence that I received in response to my articles on the university in *The Times Higher Education Supplement* helped convince me that many others shared my concerns. Discussions with friends in the United States suggested that institutional dumbing down was not merely a British problem. An important conference on the Public Intellectual organized by the Institute of Ideas in London during the summer of 2003 helped reorient this study towards an exploration of the wider question of cultural politics.

Throughout the course of writing this book I received constant feedback and criticism from Josie Appleton. For better or worse, she is responsible for the direction of many of my arguments. I also gained many insights from the input made by two Institute of Ideas stalwarts, Tiffany Jenkins and Claire Fox. My colleague Professor Mary Evans, who was completing her *Death of the University* has helped share the pain. Jenny Bristow helped to turn the manuscript into a more readable text. I am grateful to Anthony Haynes my editor at Continuum, for his generous support throughout all stages of this project.

Introduction

A Personal Journey through the Land of the Philistines

Philistine: A person deficient in liberal culture; one whose interests are material and commonplace.[1]

Unexpected circumstances provoked me to write this book. In May 2001 I wrote an article 'What is university for now?' for *The Sunday Times*, in which I raised some of my concerns about the direction of the British university. The article focused on the relative absence of intellectual stimulation and challenge on contemporary campuses. I related stories told to me by undergraduates who were profoundly bored by their university experience, and pointed out that in many cases, students could spend an entire year at university without reading a whole book.

A day after the publication of this article, I received an irate email from a senior university manager. This person was clearly incensed by my comments and accused me of 'deliberately' confusing the issues. After reading the first few angry lines I was expecting him to accuse me of fabricating my claim that undergraduates could spend a year without reading a book – but that was not the focus of his objection. He had no problem with the estrangement of undergraduates from the world of books; rather, he was angry about my arrogant assumption that books should have a privileged status in higher education. 'The tone of

[1] The Shorter Oxford Dictionary (1963), p. 1487.

the article was to suggest that you can dismiss as undemanding any programme in which students do not read "whole books"', he complained. As far as he was concerned, the book has become an optional extra resource for the present-day undergraduate.

In the months that followed this exchange, his quotation marks around 'whole books' continued to prey on my thoughts. I had anticipated a measure of hostility to the article but I did not expect a leading academic manager to treat the study of books in such a cavalier manner. Until this email exchange, I believed that despite differences over pedagogy and scholarship, the higher education establishment shared some of my misgivings and was likely to feel uncomfortable, if not embarrassed, by the evident banalization of university life. I took the view that the marginalization of intellectual passion in higher education was the unintended consequence of a new ethos of managerialism that dominates intellectual and cultural life, and was not expecting the upfront celebration of philistinism, as exemplified by my correspondent's in-your-face disparagement of studying books.

Yet I did not have to look very hard to realize that this was not the eccentric response of a maverick university administrator. Far from being defensive, the current cultural elite regards any preoccupation with the routinization of intellectual life as an object worthy of its collective scorn. Meanwhile, the behaviour of this elite is dictated by instrumentalism – an ethos that values art, culture and education insofar as they serve as instruments for serving a wider practical purpose.

Individual scholars pursuing their passionate interests increasingly risk labels such as 'irrelevant', 'elitist', 'out-of-touch' and 'marginal'. Scholarship, the pursuit of excellence and truth, is frequently represented as a bizarre, self-indulgent and irrelevant pursuit. 'A bit dodgy' is how Charles Clarke, the British Secretary of State for Education, has described the idea of education for its own sake, while asserting that his government has no interest in supporting 'the medieval concept of a community of scholars seeking truth'. Clarke's depiction of the aspiration for knowledge as an irrelevant form of medieval prejudice is testimony to the philistine ethos that informs much of educational and cultural policy today.

Such attitudes are not confined to British society or to politicians of any particular party. Clarke's Tory predecessors were no less convinced that the main purpose of education was to act as engines of economic growth. Even at the best of times, the pursuit of ideas for their own sake was an ideal that was rarely realized in practice. But at least it was an ideal that was outwardly valued by significant sections of society. Today, it is increasingly at odds with the instrumentalist ethos of global culture. 'There is a growing perception, both among students and in the university, that the humanities and languages are unnecessary indulgences', observed Vrinda Nabar, former head of the English Literature department of Mumbai University in India.[2] So too in the United States. Between 1970 and 1995, the number of foreign language majors in universities declined by 37 per cent.

Of course philistine attitudes towards education, art and culture are not a peculiarly novel development. Some of the great nineteenth-century thinkers – Mathew Arnold, Nietzsche, Goethe, Marx – were sensitive to the way in which the impersonal force of the market impinged on the development of art and culture. However, today, the influence of philistinism is not contingent on the pragmatic routines demanded by economic realities. Philistine influences are not only directed at education and culture from the outside – they have become institutionalized at the highest level of policy-making. There is a new breed of university managers, museum and gallery directors and 'know-

---

[2] See Shabnam Minwalla 'Commerce is the mantra of the moment in city colleges', *Education Times*, September 2003. *www.educationtimes.com/ arts.htm*

ledge' entrepreneurs who regard the content of culture and ideas with indifference. Their concern is to use culture to achieve an objective that is quite separate from its inner content.

The contempt that Charles Clarke displayed towards the idea of 'scholars seeking truth' expresses the temper of our times. Such cynical attitudes are underpinned by a consensus that regards the possibility of discovering the truth with scepticism. In previous times, the claim to pursue the truth sometimes covered up a variety of misdeeds. What passed for the truth were sometimes ideologies designed to serve the purposes of vested interests. But at least truth was valued for its own sake. For Aristotle, truth was the object of science: 'Philosophy is the science which considers truth.' For Albert Einstein, 'the search for truth' was 'more precious than its possession'. Rosa Luxemburg was equally passionate about the search for the truth. 'But this much I know, that it is our duty, if we desire to teach truth, to teach it wholly or not at all, to teach it clearly and bluntly, unenigmatically, unreservedly, inspired with full confidence in its powers', she told her audience. It is this passionate search for the truth that has inspired generations of thinkers during the era of modernity.

Unfortunately, contemporary culture regards the truth as a subject worthy of fiction rather than of intellectual pursuit. It is frequently argued that there is no such thing as the truth. Instead of the truth, people are exhorted to accept different opinions as representing many truths. Michel Foucault's claim that there is 'no truly universal truth' has gained widespread influence in academic circles. Truth is rarely represented as an objective fact; it is frequently portrayed as the product of subjective insight, which is in competition with other equally valid perspectives. Relativism – a perspective that contends that conceptions of truth and moral values are not absolute but are relative to the persons or groups holding them – has acquired a commanding influence over cultural life. The view that truth is in the eye of the beholder has had a significant impact on the workings of educational and cultural institutions. If the truth is relegated to the status of subjective outlook and interpretation, it ceases to be a subject of fundamental importance. It is certainly not a matter of life and death. Nor can its discovery serve as the principal justification of any significant institution. Once truth is interpreted as a dubious claim in competition with many others, it ceases to play a key role in a society's cultural life.

The demotion of the status of the truth has had significant impact on contemporary cultural life. Classical insights into the status of art – 'beauty is truth and truth is beauty' – appear inconsistent with an ethos that can only conceive of truth in the plural form. Intellectual life too must also undergo serious modification. As one important study of the role of the university remarked, 'liberal higher education has rested on the assumption that objective knowledge and truth are attainable' – before adding that 'this assumption has recently been put in doubt with modern developments in philosophy, such as relativism, critical theory and post-structuralism'. According to Ron Barnett, the author of this study, 'this amounts to an epistemological undermining of higher education'.[3] At the very least, the meaning of higher education becomes transformed once its claim to providing a pathway to the truth has been undermined.

The cavalier orientation towards the truth is also evident in relation to the wider manifestations of cultural life. The best that society can offer is now far from evident. Culture with a capital C has given way to cultures, and any claim to authority or special status is treated with derision. The conventional distinction between high and low culture makes little sense in an environment where truth has such an elusive quality. The former British Culture Secretary, Chris Smith, echoed this sentiment when he declared that the distinction between 'high

---

[3]   Barnett (1990), p. X.

culture' and 'low culture' is a misleading one and that 'George Benjamin and Noel Gallagher are both musicians of the first rank'.

Throughout the human experience culture authority has rested on the claim to represent truth. Today such sentiments tend to be treated with scepticism. Indeed, such claims are frequently castigated as elitist, and the aspiration to excellence and high standards is dismissed as a foolish lament for a golden age. Elitism, which once meant justifying a monopoly of economic, cultural and political power through the self-conscious disparagement of the people, has been redefined as the act of valuing certain aspects of culture above others. It is striking that such views tend to influence almost the entire spectrum of opinion. It is not simply the so-called cultural left that dismisses objective knowledge – the cultural elites themselves are reluctant to affirm any transcendental cultural values and truths. Instead of affirming their authority, the cultural elites appear more interested in appearing relevant, accessible and in touch with popular opinion.

Knowledge without meaning

It is paradoxical that cynicism about objective knowledge coincides with the widely held view that we live in a Knowledge Society in which it is often observed that 'knowledge is power'. Commentators frequently declare the need to respond to the demands of a Knowledge Economy, while the expansion of higher education and other cultural initiatives are justified on the grounds that they are needed for the development of a Knowledge Society. Universities and other educational institutions are regularly promoted on the grounds that they are vital for economic progress. In July 2003, the Bank of England's monetary policy committee declared that Cambridge and Oxford universities play a 'vital role in the United Kingdom economy'.[4] In the US, successive administrations have treated knowledge as a weapon vital to the nation's security.

Precisely at a time when the intellectual authority of knowledge is widely questioned, education and learning have assumed an unprecedented significance. The public is continually exhorted to become lifelong learners and to acquire new knowledge. Business and public institutions constantly avow their commitment to expanding their knowledge base. Knowledge has become a brand embraced by virtually every significant institution. But, unfortunately, the contemporary imagination endows knowledge with a superficial, almost banal, character. Often knowledge is conceptualized as a ready-made digestible product that can be 'delivered', 'transmitted', 'marketed' and 'consumed'. Mary Evans likens the academic institution to the catering industry where students receive the correct 'portion'. The transformation of knowledge into a product deprives it of any intrinsic value or meaning, and the knowledge that is peddled by the merchants of the Knowledge Economy is in fact a mundane caricature of itself. Why? Because without a relationship to Truth, knowledge has no intrinsic meaning. It becomes an abstract insight that is more likely to be transmitted than valued, and can be recycled in its most mundane form.

When knowledge is regarded as a product, its relationship to its own cultural and intellectual origin becomes indistinct. Knowledge is increasingly seen as the product of a technical process rather than of human intellectual work. For this reason, the postmodernist Jean-François Lyotard could claim the imminent 'death of the professor'. Lyotard noted that a professor is 'no more competent than memory bank networks in transmitting established knowledge'.[5] At a time when it has

---

[4] See 'Oxbridge told to modernise', BBC News: 15 July 2003.
[5] Lyotard (1984), p. 53.

become quiet fashionable to declare the 'death of the author', the 'death of the book' or the 'death of the subject', the relationship between knowledge and its intellectual origin becomes less and less clear.

The cult of the banal

During the past two centuries, the authority of intellectuals was underwritten by the belief that the pursuit of knowledge and truth merited the affirmation of society. This belief endowed intellectual work with a unique significance and provided intellectuals with an intense sense of purpose towards their mission. Indeed within the humanist tradition, intellectual and contemplative activity was represented as the highest form of human endeavour, and it was often claimed that it was this endeavour that distinguished the human from the animal.

Today, this lofty image of the intellectual appears inconsistent with the way that society regards the pursuit of knowledge. Scepticism about the possibility of objective knowledge has not only had an impact on the institution of higher education, it also has had a significant influence on intellectual life in general. If there is nothing special about knowledge, its pursuit becomes a meaningless ritual. In turn, the diminishing significance attached to knowledge has important implications for how intellectuals are regarded and how they regard themselves. In previous times, the heroic self-image of the intellectual with its extravagant pretensions was rightly mocked by satirists and critics – George Orwell, for example, gave a trenchant critique of his intellectual contemporaries. Yet despite his criticism of intellectual slothfulness, Orwell retained his belief that ideas had the power to help create a better world. Often the very force of the criticism directed at intellectuals represented an acknowledgement of the force of ideas. In the twenty-first century, by contrast, the heroic image of the classical intellectual has given way to a more down-to-earth pragmatic person, whose job is not a particularly important one. This devaluation of the role of the intellectual is intimately linked to current attitudes towards knowledge. If the search for knowledge no longer excites the cultural imagination, it is inevitable that the status of the intellectual will also cease to possess its special unique qualities.

A depressingly pedestrian account of intellectual life is regularly transmitted in discussions on this subject. The classical ideal of the search for truth associated with the intellectual has given way to one in which the pursuit of ideas is bereft of any lofty purpose. A sceptical attitude towards the role of the intellectual is not confined to the stereotypical know-nothing populist philistine. Many intellectuals have internalized the pragmatism associated with their activities, and insist that there is nothing special that defines them. This complacent attitude towards the role of the intellectual also influences academic writing on the subject. 'Perhaps it's time that someone wrote an essay entitled "Intellectuals are ordinary"', observed the Cambridge University historian Stefan Collini. Collini's aspiration to demystify the role of the intellectual very much reflects a culture that finds it difficult to endow the pursuit of ideas with very much meaning. Collini explains what he means by 'ordinary':

> 'Ordinary' in the sense that they are indeed part of the cultural landscape of all complex societies; ordinary in the sense that it is neither unthinkable nor shocking to recognize that the noun 'intellectual' might regularly be applied to some of one's friends or one's colleagues or even, in some circumstances, oneself; and above all, ordinary in the sense that carrying on the activities characteristic of intellectuals should not be seen as exceptionally heroic or exceptionally difficult or exceptionally glamorous or – and I realize here I particularly lay myself open to misunderstanding – even

exceptionally important. Important, yes, but not exceptionally important.[6]

It could be argued that there is always a case for demystifying the
sacred aura that often surrounded intellectual work. Nowadays,
however, such a project amounts to little more than kicking
against an open door. The work of today's intellectual is rarely
represented as 'exceptionally heroic', and rendering intellectual
work banal simply reinforces the low expectations that surrounds
intellectual and cultural life.

There is little doubt that intellectuals can be pompous,
arrogant and full of hot air. That is why their pretensions have
often been the target of people's humour and scorn. But such
defects of character notwithstanding, the work of the intellectual
is very important. Without a mission, a project or a desire to
uphold and promote knowledge with a capital K, intellectuals
must of course feel uneasy and constrained; and in such
circumstances the loss of authority, underwritten by engagement
with the pursuit of the truth, must have a major impact on
intellectual life. Unfortunately, these circumstances only help
breed yet more complacency and conformism.

The sociology of dumbing down

At a time when hundreds of undistinguished European towns and
cities fiercely compete with one another to win the title of 'city of
culture', it may appear mean-spirited to write about the rise of
philistinism. Cultural events and festivals are mushrooming
throughout the United States and the rest of the Western world,
and every sleepy town seems to possess a museum or at least a
heritage centre. The claim that society is dumbing down is angrily

---

[6]   See Stefan Collini ' "Every fruit juice drinker, nudist, sandal wearer ...".
Intellectuals as Other People' in Small (2002), p. 221.

dismissed by defenders of the cultural status quo, who promote what they perceive as a thriving knowledge ecology. Inevitably they point to the growth in the numbers of books published, the increase in the number of bookshops, the thriving network of book clubs or the large numbers of people attending concerts, art galleries and museums. According to one American observer:

> Externally after all, the life of the mind has seldom seemed healthier in America than it does right now. Magazines, newspaper sections, and Web sites dedicated to the doings of scholars, publishers, and writers have proliferated in the last ten years or so. In college and university towns across America, traditional and cutting-edge forms of cultural life flourish side by side. Readings, debates, and poetry slams draw hundreds. Even after college, intellectual life goes on.[7]

Education has certainly acquired a formidable influence over society. More and more people are participating in higher education. And it seems that people's involvement in education never stops. Everybody appears to be getting some kind of workplace training, or taking a pause while they are retraining. People in their forties are returning to university, or entering for the first time. We are all supposed to be lifelong learners and thousands of institutions exist to cater to every one of our knowledge needs. There is little doubt that we take education and culture seriously. We don't live in a Dark Age where it is impossible to find stimulating and challenging literature. We continue to innovate – sometimes individual artists produce magnificent art, and some intellectuals continue to develop important ideas in the humanities, social and natural sciences.

Cultural pessimists are often not able to refute the establishment's claim that we live in a flourishing knowledge society.

---

[7]   Anthony Grafton, 'The Public Intellectual and the American University', *American Scholar*, Autumn 2001.

They point to the rise of reality television at the expense of quality drama and factual programming, the growth of self-indulgent opinion columns in newspapers at the expense of thoughtful news analysis, and the steady erosion of standards at all levels of education. Such criticisms are not without foundation. But not every new project is a Millennium Dome – a testimony to cultural illiteracy. We also have the Wallace Collection or the Guggenheim Museum in Bilbao. Important innovations and institutions able to promote standards of excellence have always been a rarity. So what has changed?

The reason why the metaphor of dumbing down captures the temper of our times has little to do with the current level of cultural, artistic or educational standards. Dumbing down is fuelled by powerful forces that treat knowledge and culture as merely the means for the realization of a wider and higher objective. It is an orientation that is defined by a dogmatic commitment to instrumentalism. Such an orientation is not new – the tension between the demands of the market and economic calculation, and the pursuit of ideas or art for their own sake, has been a recurring theme in cultural debates for over two centuries. Throughout this time, artistic and intellectual endeavour has been seen as driven by interests that directly contradict the instrumentalist ethos of the market. The tension between the two was clearly formulated by Talcott Parsons, probably the most influential American sociologist of the twentieth century: 'The professional man is not thought of as engaging in the pursuit of his personal profit, but in performing services to his clients, or to impersonal values like the advancement of science.'[8]

The age-old tension between economic calculation, and a commitment to impersonal and non-instrumental values such as the advancement of knowledge and science, has meant that the intellectual and the artist were historically in a state of creative

[8]   Parsons (1954), p. 186.

conflict with the rest of society. Indeed, what was distinct and valued about artistic and intellectual activity was precisely that it was not directly dominated by an instrumental ethos. Artists and intellectuals did not set out to produce what the customer wanted, but sought to realize a loftier objective. In practice the line that divided self-interest from the disinterested pursuit of knowledge was often breached, but nevertheless the rhetoric of pursuing ideas for their own sake informed the project of the intellectual.

It is worth noting that even societies that wholeheartedly subscribed to the virtues of the market, for example the United States and Britain, continued to affirm values associated with intellectual and artistic endeavour. It was recognized that such efforts were valuable in their own right rather than because they had a high price tag attached to them. For their part – with greater or lesser effectiveness – artists and intellectuals defended their efforts because they were convinced that what they were doing was valuable in its own right.

It is only in recent times that the instrumentalist ethos has managed to dominate the way society perceives its artistic and intellectual activities. There are a number of interconnected and mutually reinforcing influences that account for this development, some of which will be further explored in the following chapters. One reason for this development is the cumulative impact of Western society's disenchantment with the legacy of the Enlightenment. As noted previously, if knowledge and the pursuit of the truth can no longer claim to make a big difference, the authority of the intellectual becomes discounted. In such circumstances the claims to intellectual autonomy, artistic integrity or disinterested professionalism become highly suspect. Once the special status that the Enlightenment tradition assigned to knowledge becomes discredited, it becomes difficult to endow intellectual and artistic activity with any special and intrinsic meaning. Such activities are represented as careers that are not

qualitatively different from other occupations. In such circumstances knowledge and art are not likely to be valued for
themselves, but because of their usefulness for society.

If knowledge and art lack any inner meaning, the reaffirmation
that they ought to be valued for their own sake can appear as a
form of special pleading. The demand to uphold certain
intellectual or artistic standards also appears inconsistent with
the absence of any agreed criteria for measuring those achievements. In any case it is not the content of ideas and art that are
valued but their utility. Consequently, how knowledge and art
are regarded is determined, not by criteria that are internal to
themselves, but by their utility for some other purpose. In such
circumstances knowledge and art serve as instruments of
economic advance, social engineering, giving communities an
identity, or providing therapy for the individual. The triumph of
this instrumentalist approach is underwritten by the inability of
contemporary society to endow intellectual and artistic work
with meaning. So while we still produce good art and books, we
find it difficult to value them in their own terms.

Why should the triumph of instrumentalism lead to dumbing
down? If we cannot value intellectual and cultural achievements
in their own terms, it becomes difficult to discriminate between
them. Claims to excellence sound self-serving if not mendacious,
and are frequently dismissed as a despicable attempt by an elite to
protect its privileges. That is why the term 'standards' has
acquired the connotation of privilege and elitism – to the extent
that in many circumstances, the insistence on upholding a
particular standard is represented as a form of institutionalized
discrimination.

Debates about educational standards are invariably terminated
with the argument that those who demand to uphold past
practices are indifferent to meeting the needs of students today.
The cultural elite does not so much call for the abandonment of
the standard of excellence. Rather, it subordinates the main-

tenance of such standards to the imperative of utility. It is the priority assigned to the utility of art and education over its inner content that continually fuels the tendency towards dumbing down. Once the inner content of art and knowledge ceases to have a socially accepted meaning, then standards become negotiable, and easily subordinated to pragmatic and instrumentalist concerns. In her first speech as Minister of State of the Arts at the Cheltenham Literature Festival, Baroness Tessa Blackstone asked: 'Can the arts be more than just frivolous, trivial, irrelevant?' Her answer was yes, but only if they can be used for purposes other than aesthetic ones. For Blackstone the arts are important because apparently they improve employability, eradicate inequality and help prevent crime. '[I have] no doubt that the arts can contribute to improving health outcomes', she added.

In previous times the dumbing down of culture was classically the result of the operation of the market on intellectual life. Back in the 1930s, F. R. Leavis pointed the finger at the commercial imperative for the massification of culture. The commercial imperative is no less significant today than in the past. But today it is not market forces that are primarily responsible for the process of dumbing down. Rather, it is a direct consequence of public policy that promotes the politics of inclusion at any cost. Why this should be the case will be explored in Chapter 5.

Negotiating standards

In the numerous controversies that surround standards, be they about education, art, speech or political life, not even the most vulgar cultural entrepreneur demands abandoning standards of excellence. Instead, those who sneer at the word 'standards' believe that there are many different modes of defining and affirming excellence. The so-called Culture Wars in the US and the incessant debate over educational standards in the UK are symptomatic of a climate where competitive claims-making influences the representation of standards. A standard with a capital S is inconsistent with the mood of contemporary culture. Any claim that privileges a particular art form, way of speaking, or educational achievement, is dismissed on the grounds that they possess no special merit over and above those achieved in different circumstances by other people and other cultures. Moreover, the act of upholding a standard in order to make judgements of value is sometimes depicted as an act of symbolic violence against people from a different cultural background. According to one such account: 'excellence is an intellectual, cultural and social construction that not only represents social inequalities through its reflective practices, but as well, arbitrariness as a characteristic of its construction'.[9]

The flourishing of relativist critiques of truth and knowledge has been facilitated by the reluctance of the contemporary cultural elite to uphold and clearly define standards. It has no fundamental principles to uphold and accepts no responsibility for forging a consensus around what ought to constitute the achievement of excellence. Since the very notion of a standard is depicted as elitist, it feels uneasy about promoting clearly defined ideals. It is happy to turn an institution like the BBC into an all-purpose medium that self-consciously professes to be flexible on this subject. Individuals within the cultural elites may have a clear view on the subject of what standards society ought to aspire to achieve, but as a collective entity they experience standards as a potential source of conflict and controversy. Consequently the cultural elite regards the maintenance of standards as at best a mixed blessing and at worst an obstacle to avoid.

The growing scepticism towards standards is most striking in discussions about assessing achievement. It is not unusual to hear

---

[9]   Romero, A. (1998), 'Educational change and discourse communities: representing change in post modern times', *Curriculum Studies* 6, p. 53.

members of the UK educational establishment explain that the examination system is elitist and discriminates against the intellectual skill acquired by working-class people. In a similar way, museums, galleries and even libraries have been criticized for not valuing the skills of people from different backgrounds. From a relativistic perspective, the very attempt to measure achievement according to common standards is likely to be discriminatory, if not oppressive.

Different cultures and experiences have a lot to contribute to the development of human civilization. But the targeting of standards has little to do with an enlightened appreciation of human culture. Hostility towards a Standard with a capital S is often fuelled by the belief that the effort and expectation that it embodies is beyond the capacity of most people. This sentiment is most striking in education, where there are desperate attempts made to ensure that people achieve some kind of a qualification. As a result standards are continuously reconfigured to ensure that students succeed. Grade inflation and the devaluation of diplomas and degrees only increase the appetite for further fiddling with the mode of assessment. Policy-makers no longer pretend to endow standards with any objective existence – they have simply become the tools of social policy. Some advocates of this approach even go so far as to identify such 'inclusive' policies as a form of best practice. 'We contend that being inclusive is one measure of educational excellence' argue advocates of 'inclusive education'.[10]

Today's manipulative attitude towards standards is in part a product of disappointment with the experience of reform in education, culture and social policy. Attempts to provide equal opportunities to all sections of society have not led to the

---

[10] Nunan, T., Rigmor, George and McCausland, H. (2000), 'Inclusive education in universities: why it is important and how it might be achieved', *International Journal of Inclusive Education* 4(1), p. 70.

elimination of privilege serving as a passport to success. As a result there is widespread unease about the relationship between effort and achievement. Instead of exploring why mobility based on merit has had only a limited success, the tendency is to write off the meritocratic ideal altogether. Pessimism now shapes contemporary views towards the meritocratic ideal, which tends to be denounced as an apology for the success of those with accumulated privilege while others are consigned to a life of failure.

From meritocracy to mediocracy

The most striking manifestation of a cavalier approach towards aspiring to standards of excellence is a growing tendency to dismiss the meritocratic ideal as an impossible con trick. The meritocratic ideal claimed that through the provision of equality of opportunity, the most able individuals would be able to rise to the top of society. The principle of merit would replace reliance of inheritance and family ties as the main instrument of social advance. The meritocratic ideal did not simply provide a linkage between individual effort and success – it also held out the promise of cumulative development through harnessing the provision of equality of opportunity to the achievement of the highest standards. As such, it can also be understood as an attempt to achieve the highest possible cultural standards through giving a free rein to the flourishing of merit.

There are considerable obstacles to people of different backgrounds having an opportunity to exercise their talents and realize their potential. Privilege and wealth provide the new generation with unfair advantage and make it difficult for others to rise to the top. But despite all the obstacles that stood in the way of its realization, it was felt that the meritocratic ideal was worth fighting for. Today, by contrast, there is a sharp decline in the enthusiasm for the principle of promoting achievement through merit. The ideal of merit, like that of a standard, is often portrayed as an act of deception designed by a dishonest elite in order to fool the people.

A powerful school of thought used to believe that the democratization of education and culture is compatible with the maintenance, indeed the rise, of standards. Yet in recent years, this idea has taken a severe knock. Those disposed towards traditional elitist ideals have always believed that the democratization of education and culture was inconsistent with the maintenance of excellence in intellectual life. Today, this current of opinion still persists, but is rarely expressed in open form. In today's political climate the democratization of education and culture is rarely questioned. Almost every institution possesses a mission statement that sets out the widening of participation as one of its principal objectives. It is not the democratization of culture that is interrogated today, but the attempt to preserve or raise educational or cultural standards. And the reason why the desirability of upholding standards is put to question by advocates of widening participation is because they, like the traditional elitists, genuinely do not believe that the democratization of cultural life can be reconciled with standards of excellence.

In a roundabout way, today's cultural leaders accept the traditional elitist diagnosis but draw radically different conclusions. They want democracy but are prepared to be flexible about the maintenance of standards. While they may not come out and say this, cultural leaders claim that the project of maintaining high standards is elitist and inherently anti-democratic. That is why arguments that seek to promote excellence in art, culture and education are frequently dismissed as an elitist attempt to turn the clock back to the days when only a tiny minority could have access to cultural capital.

The aim of this book is to question the pessimistic assumption that portrays popular participation as inconsistent with the maintenance of standards of excellence. I argue that the internalization of this perspective by today's cultural elite has led to a flourishing of philistinism and an unhealthy instrument-alism towards intellectual life; and that, furthermore, participa-tion without the maintenance of standards represents a fraud inflicted on millions of people, which disorients society from realizing its potential in the century ahead. This book is devoted to promoting the project of developing society's intellectual and cultural life through the development of an educated public.

The merit of merit

One of the central arguments advanced against the maintenance of standards of excellence is that this is an elitist project that will exclude the vast majority from participating in institutions of culture. This pessimistic conclusion is based on the premise that the public lacks the resources to benefit from demanding forms of cultural and educational experience. As a result, it is argued that standards and expectations will have to change in order to facilitate widening participation. This sceptical assessment of people's abilities has encouraged a mood of hostility towards the idea of rewarding people according to their merit.

Suspicion of standards and merit go hand in hand. It is worth noting that Michael Young's *The Rise of the Meritocracy* (1958), a classical attack on the meritocratic ideal, caricatures a meritocratic statement as: 'no longer is it so necessary to debase standards by attempting to extend a higher civilization to the children of the lower classes'. This association of reactionary elitism with concern about people debasing standards has become part of the collective wisdom of the cultural elite. That is why proposals to select individuals based on merit, the testing of children and adolescents, or the making of judgements of value about art, are often criticized as unfair and elitist.

In economic life, the anti-meritocratic consensus is particularly concerned with the potential for widening economic inequality fuelled by the attitude 'winner takes all'. In relation to wider cultural life, anti-meritocratic sentiment is focused on a preoccupation with failure and the need to immunize people from regarding themselves as failures. 'Every selection of one is a rejection of the many', warns Michael Young's anti-hero.[11] Quarantining the public from a sense of rejection is right at the top of the mission statement of the anti-meritocratic movement.

Of course the meritocratic ideal is rarely realized in practice. Intellectual and cultural life is riddled with discrimination and inequalities. Although many outward forms of discrimination have been eliminated, we are far from achieving a world where individuals can compete on a level playing field. The accident of birth still exercises a decisive role in determining people's life chances. But does the failure to realize the meritocratic ideal represent an argument against it? Or does it, as I believe, represent an argument for reflecting on what went wrong, in order to formulate policies that can eliminate the obstacles that prevent the exercise of individual abilities? Critics of meritocracy in intellectual and cultural life are not seriously engaged with this question. Their main concern is with preventing people from regarding themselves as failures, and this has great influence over policy-makers and the contemporary educational and cultural establishment. As I will argue, it is not so much a democratic impulse that fuels the contemporary rejection of meritocracy, but a therapeutic concern with avoiding feelings of rejection within the wider public.

To put it bluntly, many critics of meritocracy believe that meritocracy leads to mental illness. Testing and selection are said to breed failure and rejection, which in turn are held responsible for the lowering of people's self-esteem. The American social critic

[11] See Young (1961), p. 15.

Christopher Lasch argued that meritocracy has led to an 'obsessive concern' with self-esteem. He claimed that the new therapies 'seek to counter the oppressive sense of failure in those who fail to climb the educational ladder even while they leave intact the existing structure of elite recruitment – the acquisition of educational credentials.[12] There is little doubt that a mood of failure has led to the flourishing of new therapies. However, how individuals feel about themselves, how they engage with the experience of disappointment and the pressures of everyday life, is not reducible to the workings of meritocracy. Such sentiments are the product of wider social and cultural influences. If people feel rejected or lack self-respect it may well be because they are not sure where they belong or how they fit into the wider scheme of things. People can live with disappointment if they have the cultural resources that allow them to make sense of the world. What they need is not to be protected from the sense of failure, but provided with an opportunity to gain insights into their lives through exploring the very best that our culture has to offer. Rewarding merit implies treating people as adults, whereas magicking away the sense of failure is motivated by the desire to treat them as children.

The purpose of the book

This book is not a lament for a lost golden age of intellectual life, when people were smarter, the public received a higher standard of education and creativity, and a more dynamic culture prevailed. We have not turned into simpletons. There are lots of impressive works of art and science and we continue to make remarkable discoveries. In any case, whatever happened in the past is of little help in solving the challenges that we face today.

---

[12] Christopher Lasch, 'Revolt of the Elites', *Harper's Magazine*, November 1994.

In every era, society is confronted with new problems and opportunities. The aim of this book is to question how we are currently going about developing ideas, educating people and creating a new public.

Unfortunately, the debates about education, culture and the arts are dominated by two sides that both convey patronizing anti-democratic sentiments towards the human subject. There is a small minority of opinion that continues to argue that the democratization of intellectual and cultural life will inevitably lead to the decline of standards. From the standpoint of an oligarchical defence of high culture, any attempt to involve the public must lead to the triumph of a lower form of mass culture. Today, very few people are prepared to argue an unambiguous and forthright defence of such an elitist outlook. The dominant side of the debate is outwardly and self-consciously anti-elitist. It continually applauds mass participation, public dialogue and the inclusion of all voices. However, it has little faith in the ability of the public to use and benefit from the best that culture has to offer. Like the traditional elitist perspective, it believes that the people lack the capacity to benefit from standards of excellence. But instead of following the path of the old conservative elites, the new conservative imagination makes no attempt to exclude. Its objective is to transform intellectual and cultural life in order to make it hospitable for a public that cannot be expected to engage with the best. This philistine agenda patronizes the public and treats people like children that need to be protected from more disturbing cultural and intellectual challenges.

The aim of this book is to question both the anti-democratic and patronizing underpinning of contemporary education and cultural politics. Such politics not only restrain intellectual and cultural creativity – they also infantilize the public and lower its expectations. I embrace any attempt to provide the public with opportunities to engage in intellectual exploration. But I decry the paternalistic project of feeding the public with easily digestible portions of knowledge and culture. Inclusion and participation for their own sake has little merit. Flattering people – be they schoolchildren, university students, the audience in a museum – serves only the imperative of social engineering. This book argues that a precondition for expanding genuine public engagement is the provision of standards equivalent to the best that society has to offer.

Dumbing down is not an esoteric issue that concerns only academics, artists and intellectuals. The prevailing level of education, culture and intellectual debate is important for the flourishing of a democratic ethos. Intellectuals in different guises play a crucial role in initiating dialogue and engaging the curiosity and passion of the public. Today that engagement is conspicuously feeble. Unsurprisingly, the cultural elites' cynicism towards knowledge and truth has been transmitted to the people through educational and cultural institutions and the media. Apathy and social disengagement are symptoms of a culture that tends to equate debate with the banal exchange of technical opinions. Because all of this really matters, a culture war against the philistines is long overdue.

1 Devaluing the Intellect

One of the most striking manifestations of the banalization of cultural life is the transformation of the intellectual into a uniquely insignificant figure. Even in France, the supposed home of intellectuals, they appear to lead a life of cultural irrelevance. As an American commentator observed, compared to a figure such as Jean-Paul Sartre, 'Today's French intellectuals look like puny technocrats'.[1]

Intellectuals reflect their culture and the temper of their time. The role they play and the influence that they are able to wield has fluctuated over the past three centuries. This is not the first time that the intellectual is seen to have a feeble presence in society. During the 1950s, at the height of the Cold War, many leading pro-Western thinkers, especially in the United States, were concerned about the exhaustion of intellectual life. Apathy and mental fatigue appeared to afflict those involved in intellectual work. Even the media joined in the discussion and attempted to galvanize into action what it saw as a hibernating intelligentsia. According to one account:

> Throughout the 1950s, magazines and newspapers berated the young as members of a 'silent generation' – politically apathetic, intellectually passive, caring less for social causes, than for economic security, preoccupied with private lives.[2]

[1] Jim Holt, 'Jean-Paul Sartre: Brilliant Philosopher or Totalitarian Apologist?', *Slate*: 22 September 2003.
[2] Pells (1985), p. 201.

Although superficially this description of events appears to capture the mood of our era, it is important to note that the influence of the intellectual even of the 1950s' 'silent generation' was far greater than in our times. Although it is difficult to measure or compare such influence, it is possible to point to a number of important differences between the periods. The influence of intellectuals on political life, particularly on the left wing of politics, stands in marked contrast to the situation today. And yet, the very public concern with the relative absence of the voice of the intellectual was a testimony to the importance that was attached to it in the 1950s. Today the attitude that is far more likely to predominate is, 'Does it really matter?' The lack of interest in the status of the intellectual stands in sharp contrast to the passionate debates that surrounded their role in previous times.

We live in a time when books and newspaper articles with titles like *The Last Intellectual* capture a pervasive sense of intellectual disengagement. It is not simply a cultural affectation to describe some very ordinary thinkers as 'the last intellectual'[3] – there do not appear to be very many prominent intellectual voices, and it is difficult to discern their collective impact on society. Indeed, it is the absence of a significant intellectual movement devoted to the advance of a distinct set of ideas to the wider public that illustrates the mood of disengagement.

From a powerful protagonist to a lost soul

The significance of this change in the status of intellectuals can be readily grasped when placed in a historical perspective. Throughout most of the past three centuries, the intellectual

---

[3]   Such as, for example, Ella Taylor's 'The Last Intellectual: Clive James. Renaissance Man', *LA Weekly*: 17 July 2003.

possessed formidable cultural authority and influence. Commentators often had an exaggerated sense of the status of intellectuals, and they were seen to have enormous power to influence events. Intellectuals were frequently portrayed as dangerous subversives who led the assault on the traditional order and who succeeded in unleashing the dark forces of radical destruction. Enlightenment intellectuals were frequently blamed for imposing their ideology of reason on the rest of society. Burke's denunciation of men of letters, who are so 'fond of distinguishing themselves', so 'rarely averse to innovation' and so enamoured 'with their theories about the rights of man that they have totally forgot his nature', provided the prototype for the often-repeated critique of the self-indulgent and disruptive intellectual. Intellectuals were often not liked but they were taken very, very seriously.

Anti-intellectualism represented a strong current of opinion within American culture. Richard Hofstadter's *Anti-Intellectualism in America* provides a graphic account of the influence of this trend. The New England Puritan writer John Cotton warned in 1642 that 'the more learned and witty you bee, the more fit to act for Satan you will be'. Such sentiments of dislike for clever people were motivated by the fear that the intellectual was likely to transgress conventional norms.

Since Burke's time intellectuals have been blamed for virtually every ill that afflicts society. Many a right-wing critic in France blamed Marcel Proust for single-handedly causing the moral decay of the Third Republic. In Britain the Bloomsbury set were represented as the villains in the traditionalist imagination; they were blamed for sowing the seeds of doubt about Britain's imperial mission. They were portrayed as the decadent beneficiaries of Britain's greatness, who took delight in systematically destroying all the values that made up the identity of the nation. In the US, the New York intellectual was often accused of importing un-American ideas into the country. And during the

sixties and seventies, campus radicals were held responsible for
the moral decline of America.

Intellectuals were frequently denounced as treasonous para-
sites or, more charitably, as useful fools. Critics of this treachery
were motivated by the conviction that social disorder and moral
decay were the consequences of the formidable influence of
intellectual demagogues upon the gullible masses. The most
systematic exposition of the theory of the politically motivated
intellectual influencing public opinion to the detriment of society
is to be found in Julien Benda's *The Betrayal of the Intellectual*.
Published in the 1920s, this book denounces intellectuals for
abandoning their role as guardians of the truth for that of
political attachment. He accuses intellectuals of 'divinizing'
politics and of being responsible for the unleashing of political
passions. Benda claims that when intellectuals become involved
in political movements, they give coherence to passions and turn
them into pernicious ideologies. 'Our age is indeed the age of the
intellectual organization of political hatreds', writes Benda.[4] The
linkage of intellectuals with ideologies underpinned numerous
accounts of the explosive mass movements of the twentieth
century.

By the time of the Cold War, the tradition of blaming
intellectuals for political extremism and destruction was well
established. The belief that the intellectual bore a significant
responsibility for the rise of totalitarianism dominates Arthur
Koestler's 1944 article 'The Intelligentsia'. Koestler predicted that
'we are in for an era of managerial super-states' where the
intelligentsia is 'bound to become a special sector in the civil
service'.[5] Joseph Schumpeter saw the intellectual as a threat to the
survival of capitalism. In his major work of the 1940s,
Capitalism, Socialism and Democracy, he argued that the

---

[4]   Benda (1959), p. 21.
[5]   Koestler (1983), p. 84.

intellectual was responsible for establishing 'the atmosphere of hostility to capitalism'. Similar arguments were repeated in the sixties, when the prevailing sense of disorder and moral malaise was blamed on the actions of the politically motivated radical intellectual.

Denunciations of the destructive legacy of the intellectuals soon claimed that this powerful group had become, or was about to become, a new class. Bertrand de Jouvenel's Cold War polemic against the intellectual argued that it was the intelligentsia that represented the greatest threat to society: 'It has for long been assumed that the great problem of the twentieth century is that of the industrial wage-earner's place in society; insufficient notice has been taken of the rise of a vast intellectual class, whose place in society may prove the greater problem.'[6] Within a decade this argument had acquired the status of a conventional wisdom. Certainly by the 1960s no one would pause to remark that not enough attention had been paid to the role of the intellectual. Interminable discussion about how the intelligentsia had replaced the proletariat as the truly revolutionary class soon followed.

Probably the most influential text dealing with the intellectual in the 1970s and early 1980s was Alvin Gouldner's *The Future of Intellectuals and the Rise of the New Class*. Gouldner claimed that this new class was 'the most progressive force in modern society and in the center of whatever human emancipation is possible in the foreseeable future'.[7] The idea that intellectuals constituted a benign progressive elite was the mirror image of the right-wing denunciation of the new class as a parasitic destructive force. However, both standpoints credited the intellectual with considerable power to influence the course of events.

In retrospect, one is struck by the inflated significance

---

[6] B. de Jouvenel, 'Treatment of Capitalism by Intellectuals', in Hayek (1954), p. 122.
[7] Gouldner (1979), p. 83.

attached to the role of the intellectual in the past. Gouldner's caricature of the rise of a new class of intellectuals appears today as an incomprehensible anachronism. So do the passionate denunciations of the Enlightenment Intellectual. Occasionally one encounters a well-rehearsed warning of the intellectual ambition to transform the world. 'One would, however, be ill advised to assume that we have seen the last of the rage to reorder political, social, and economic relations in light of the dictates of theory', cautions one current anti-Enlightenment thinker.[8] But such warnings seem strangely dissonant with today's cultural climate.

Today few look upon the intellectual as a dangerous fanatic threatening the moral fibre of society. To be sure, there is a handful of conservative thinkers on the losing side of the Culture Wars who object to the behaviour of left-wing academics, but their focus is on university politics rather than on the intellectual. Indeed the target is often the mendacious university administrator or bureaucrat rather than the intellectual. Here and there anti-intellectual sentiments still prevail, but they lack a clear focus and do not provoke any serious debate. Insofar as there is any contemporary discussion about the intellectual, it is motivated by concern about what has happened to this figure. In the past, the question 'where are the intellectuals?' could be answered by pointing to a variety of geographical areas – Paris, Berlin, Vienna, St Petersburg, Bloomsbury, Greenwich Village – as sites of intellectual ferment. Today, one would be hard pushed to point to such a place, and campus towns are inhabited by intelligent and well-educated people who work as professional academics rather than as participants in an intellectual milieu.

Intellectuals are rarely represented as having the power to do very much. The most controversial text on the question of the

---

[8]   Paul A. Rahe, 'The Idea of the Public Intellectual in the Age of the Enlightenment', in Melzer, Weinberger and Zinman (eds) (2003), p. 46.

intellectual in recent years is probably Russell Jacoby's *The Last Intellectuals*. This book explores the disappearance of the intellectual from public life and attempts to analyse the causes of the intellectual's diminishing impact upon society. The very fact that today many monographs ask 'what is a public intellectual?' suggests that what they are describing corresponds to an endangered species. With questions posed like 'who are they?' and 'where are they?', it is worth reminding ourselves just what we mean by the concept of an intellectual.

What makes the Intellectual?

Intellectuals are often defined according to their occupations. It is sometimes suggested that people who work with their brains are doing intellectual work – therefore in Western societies, where an ever-decreasing proportion of the population work with their hands, millions of people perform intellectual labour. In addition to obvious candidates like teachers, lawyers and scientists, there is a veritable army of public sector and private sector employees who are employed to perform mental work. However, those involved in non-manual occupations are not necessarily intellectuals. As Ron Eyerman argues, it is important to distinguish between the performance of intellectual labour and intellectuals, because intellectuals' identity 'forms around other kinds of interests than those related to social position'.[9] Intellectuals are not defined according to the jobs they do but the manner in which they act, the way they see themselves, and the values that they uphold.

Being an intellectual is not about how one makes a living. Coser argues that intellectuals 'live for rather than off ideas.' Eyerman echoes this point when he states that 'intellectuals may

[9]   Eyerman (1994), p. 6.

live off their ideas but they must also live for them'.[10] Although the notion of living for an idea may strike the reader as hopelessly idealistic, it has motivated the behaviour of millions of people during recent centuries. Indeed, it can be said that whatever reservation one has about such idealism, it has inspired many to see creative possibilities beyond the sober realities of everyday existence. Even being an academic expert does not lead directly to becoming an intellectual. As the French sociologist Pierre Bourdieu commented, in order to 'claim the title of intellectual', cultural producers 'must deploy their specific expertise and authority in their particular cultural domain in a political activity outside it'.[11] From Bourdieu's standpoint, someone like Einstein exercises intellectual authority when he steps outside his expert field (physics) and comments on the state of global politics. Their sense of identity as an intellectual derives, in part, from participating in a project that transcends any particular occupation or interest. 'The intentional meaning of "being an intellectual" is to rise above the partial preoccupation of one's own profession or artistic *genre* and engage with the global issues of truth, judgement and taste of the time', argues Bauman.[12] Not surprisingly, one of the values most acclaimed by intellectuals is the ability to pursue a life of independence and autonomy. Gouldner believed that autonomy represents a key aspiration for intellectuals, observing that the 'deepest structure in the culture and ideology of intellectuals is their pride in their own *autonomy*'.[13] The desire to possess the freedom to act in accordance with one's belief and reflection strongly motivates the behaviour of the intellectual. That is why intellectuals often exist in a state of creative tension with the rules and restrictions imposed by the prevailing institutions on everyday life.

[10]   Coser (1965), p. viii and Eyerman (1994), p. 13.
[11]   Bourdieu (1989), p. 99.
[12]   Bauman (1987), p. 2.
[13]   Gouldner (1979), p. 33.

To feel and behave like an intellectual requires at least a mental distancing from the conventions and pressures of everyday affairs. Eyerman noted that 'the more intellectual labour is controlled by external forces, rules and procedures, supervisors and so on, the less of an intellectual one feels oneself to be'.[14] The aspiration for autonomy is driven by the understanding that ideas cannot be developed in accordance with a schedule or the dictates of a particular institution. It is generally recognized that a degree of detachment is essential for the gaining of perspective and of creativity. Intellectuals can be employed by institutions, but if their imagination and work remains confined to these institutions they will become simply experts and technocrats. An important American study published in the 1960s argued that if intellectuals were absorbed into the 'establishment', this 'would spell the end of intellectuals as recent history has known them'. The author warned that such a development would not serve the interests of America, since 'only if intellectuals preserve critical intelligence, maintain some remoteness from day-to-day tasks, and cultivate concern with ultimate rather than with proximate values can they serve society fully'.[15]

Even in the most favourable periods for cultural development, intellectuals tend to have an uneasy relationship with the status quo. There are, of course, mandarin intellectuals who serve the dominant oligarchy. But such mandarins quickly turn into ideologues and apologists and become alienated from intellectual pursuits. They swiftly compromise their authority as intellectuals. It is difficult to envisage how intellectual work can be advanced in a way that is entirely conformist. Both conservative and radical intellectuals interpret the world through the prism of principles that are in a state of permanent tension with the practical affairs of society. One group criticizes the prevailing state of affairs in

---

[14] Eyerman (1994), p. 12.
[15] Cited in Coser (1965), pp. 358–9.

order to move society backward, and the other to transform certain aspects of it.

The creative role of an intellectual requires detachment from any particular identity and interest. Since the beginning of modernity, the authority of the intellectual has rested on the claim to be acting and speaking on behalf of society as a whole. The intellectual can be seen as the personification of the Enlightenment legacy and has traditionally sought to represent the standpoint of universality. Through their embrace of universalism, modern intellectuals 'have constituted themselves as they are in and by their rejection of particularism', observes Pierre Bourdieu.[16] Through speaking for values that transcend specific experience – reason, rationality, science, freedom – intellectuals reaffirm the salience of the Enlightenment project.

Regardless of individual temperament, intellectuals are often forced to challenge contemporary wisdom and convention. The potential for such conflict is contained within the universalist perspective, which contradicts the customs and conventions pragmatically constructed to guide the life of particular groups. As Edward Said noted, acting on the principles of universalism is a risky business. 'Universality means taking a risk in order to go beyond the easy certainties provided us by our background, language, nationality, which so often shields us from the reality of others.'[17] It is because intellectuals of a universalist persuasion often raise disturbing questions about prevailing customs and assumptions that they are often perceived as unpatriotic cosmopolitan outsiders. Orwell's criticism of intellectuals who are 'ashamed of their nationality' is paradigmatic in this respect.[18] The detached individual, who does not quite conform to the prevailing norms, was a part of the stereotype of the twentieth-century intellectual.

---

[16] Bourdieu (1989), p. 110.
[17] Said (1994), p. xii
[18] See Orwell 1941), pp. 46–8.

Not all intellectuals subscribe to the philosophical and political outlook of the Enlightenment. Over the years, conservative intellectuals have been animated by their distaste for Enlightenment values. But in the very act of seeking to uphold their version of tradition against the claims of the Enlightenment, they too have had to go beyond their particular experience and adopt a more cosmopolitan outlook. Their critique is as much a product of the Enlightenment as the Enlightenment is the object of their rancour. Conservative intellectuals are no less the product of the Enlightenment than their more radical counterparts.

Being an intellectual implies social engagement. It is difficult to live for ideas and not attempt to influence society. It involves not only being involved in creative mental activity, but also the assumption of social responsibility and taking a political stand. Not every intellectual has a disposition for social engagement but, as a group, intellectuals are drawn towards political life. Regis Debray in his study of French intellectuals states that it is not the level of education that defines the intellectual but the 'project of influencing the public'. Debray characterizes this orientation as a moral project that is essentially political.[19] Such a project is not necessarily a party political one, but one that is prepared to conduct a battle for the public hearts and minds.

There are numerous definitions of the intellectual. They are sometimes depicted as the defenders of cultural standards, as a group of perpetual critics and dissenters, as the conscience of society. Lewis Coser defines intellectuals as 'men who never seem satisfied with things as they are'. But he understands that the most fruitful way of understanding intellectuals is in relation to the realm of ideas.[20] Many observers believe that one of the distinguishing features of the intellectual is his or her ability to engage with the wider issues of the day. 'The intentional meaning

---

[19] Debray (1981), p. 127.
[20] Coser (1965), p. viii.

of "being an intellectual" is to rise above the partial preoccupation of one's own profession or artistic *genre* and engage with the global issues of truth, judgement and taste of the time', argues Bauman.[21] According to Edward Said, intellectuals assume their role through representing the standpoint of a constituency or of a wider public: 'My argument is that intellectuals are individuals with a vocation for the art of representing, whether that is talking, writing, teaching, appearing on television.'[22] One of the simplest, yet most useful, definitions of the intellectual is provided by Seymour Lipset. According to Lipset, intellectuals are 'all those who create, distribute, and apply *culture*, that is, the symbolic order of man, including art, science, and religion'.[23] Whatever definition we prefer, being an intellectual involves an intimate relationship to the pursuit of ideas and of truth.

Of course intellectuals do not all share the same philosophy and political outlook. They live for different ideas. But despite differences, which are sometimes bitter and far-reaching, intellectuals share a common desire to influence the world. In particular they possess a common commitment to being the critical voice of the truth as they see it. The powerful American social commentator C. Wright Mills argued that 'in the first instance the politics of the intellectual are "the politics of truth"'. He took the view that through the pursuit of the truth, the intellectual held the powers-that-be to account. 'Whatever else the intellectual may be, surely he is among those who ask serious questions, and, if he is a political intellectual, he asks his questions of those with power.'[24]

There is little doubt that the portrait of the intellectual depicted above provides an idealized version of the workings of

---

[21]   Bauman (1987), p. 2.
[22]   Said (1994), p. 10.
[23]   Lipset (1960), p. 311.
[24]   C. Wright Mills, 'On Knowledge and Power', pp. 611–12 in Horowitz (1963).

this group. Throughout the past three centuries most intellectuals were not full-time crusaders for truth. Like anyone else, intellectuals often compromise, withdraw under pressure and conform to the cultural climate that prevails. Sometimes they can trade in their autonomy for an easy life and sometimes their idealism is merely a mask for the ruthless pursuit of self-interest. But whatever the trajectory and characteristics of individual intellectuals, as a group they have played an important role in questioning conventions and sensitizing society to ideals and values that have helped to push forward human progress.

Today, the role of critical engagement with ideas is often associated with what is sometimes described as the 'traditional intellectual'. The very fact that the word traditional is used in qualification indicates that existence of this type of person is now directly put to question. Just as Truth is often represented as lacking authority, so too people who claim to pursue it are dismissed as an anachronistic irrelevance. That is why the relevance of the role of the 'traditional critical intellectual' to today's conditions is frequently interrogated. Even commentators who are sympathetic to the exercise of intellectual authority believe that its 'traditional role has eroded'. 'Perhaps we have to re-evaluate the meaning and the importance of the category of the traditional intellectual itself as well as analyze its changing conditions' states Katrin Fridjonsdottir, a perceptive commentator on this subject.[25] So what are the influences that have made contemporary society relatively inhospitable to the survival of the so-called traditional intellectual?

[25] Katrin Fridjonsdottir (1987), 'The Modern Intellectual: In Power or Disarmed? Reflections on the Sociology of Intellectuals and Intellectual Work', in Eyerman, Svensson and Soderquist (1987), p. 113.

Contemporary society and the intellectual

Some of the structural changes associated with the decline of the traditional intellectual have been the growing impact of the market upon intellectual life, the institutionalization and the professionalization of intellectual life, the growing power of the media and the erosion of public space for the exercise of autonomy. Many writers on this subject claim that the main driving force behind the transformation of the intellectual landscape has been the relentless expansion of academia. According to this perspective, academic careerism has dealt a serious body blow to the continued vitality of intellectual life.[26]

The rise of the expert and of the professional has been a significant feature of capitalist societies for some time. Since the 1950s, this trend has become highly visible and now exercises a powerful influence on how authority is perceived. Those who portray intellectuals as a 'new class' often argue that professionalism serves as an ideology that now underpins the authority of the ruling elites. From this perspective, it is possible to draw the conclusion that intellectuals are more powerful than in previous times. This approach was systematically advanced in the 1970s by Gouldner, who claimed that 'professionalism silently installs the New Class as the paradigm of virtuous and legitimate authority, performing with technical skill and dedicated concern for society-at-large'.[27]

It is doubtful that the ascendancy of professional authority has boosted the influence of the intellectual. The mental work of the professional is focused on the provision of services, not the promotion of ideas. Insofar as ideas are involved in the delivery of a professional task, they are not valued for their own sake but as a means to their realization. It is not the performance of

[26]   This point is well argued by Jacoby (1987).
[27]   Gouldner (1979), p. 19.

intellectual labour or any specific economic function that defines intellectuals. Intellectuals are constituted through their relationship to society and the development of ideas. And whatever their occupations, it is not directly through their jobs that they exercise their role as intellectuals.

Contrary to the new class thesis, the expansion of professionalism may well create new obstacles to the pursuit of intellectual activity. Professionalism promotes values and forms of behaviour that may well be inconsistent with those of the intellectual. Activities such as offering a critique of the status quo, acting as the conscience of society, or pursuing the truth regardless of the consequences are not what the job of a professional is all about. As Katrin Fridjonsdottir remarks, a professional expert might be a critical intellectual but 'he is definitely not expected to behave like one in his role as an expert'.[28] Indeed the forms of behaviour associated with the professional expert are very different to the way that intellectuals act. That is why many writers on the subject believe that professionalism constitutes the most significant threat facing the intellectual. The inconsistency between the ethos of professionalism and that of the intellectual was spelled out by Edward Said:

> By professionalism I mean thinking of your work as an intellectual as something you do for a living, between the hours of nine and five with one eye on the clock, and another cocked at what is considered to be proper, professional behaviour – not rocking the boat, not straying outside the accepted paradigms or limits, making yourself marketable and above all presentable, hence uncontroversial and unpolitical and 'objective'.[29]

[28] Katrin Fridjonsdottir (1987), 'The Modern Intellectual: In Power or Disarmed? Reflections on the Sociology of Intellectuals and Intellectual Work', in Eyerman (1987), p. 121.

[29] Said (1994), p. 55.

Once intellectual work becomes professionalized, it ceases to possess its independence and potential for asking difficult questions of society. Instead it acquires a managerial or technocratic function.

Paradoxically, it appears that the very growth in the demand for intellectual labour has thrown up new obstacles to the exercise of intellectual activity. The flourishing of a market for ideas has encouraged the professionalization of intellectual work. And as Eyerman noted, through moving intellectual labour from the margin to the centre of society the market has acquired an unprecedented influence over the conduct of intellectual life. The result of this process has been the institutionalization of many of the functions associated with the activity of the intellectual:

> Those institutions and processes which traditionally have been formative for intellectuals – the university, the literary and political public sphere, especially as connected to cultural and class conflict – have in late modern societies become more and more institutionalized, professionalized and commercialized. The role of the social critic, so central to one traditional ideal of the intellectual, has itself been institutionalized to such an extent that the 'intellectual' has become a permanent feature on television talk shows and on the 'culture' pages of the more serious newspapers.[30]

So although intellectual work is more in evidence than in previous times, these are functions performed by institutions and their professionals rather than by intellectuals. Those intellectuals who attempt to transmit their ideas through the media often turn into talking heads servicing the show. They often find that they are tolerated only insofar as they provide sound bites and entertainment.

The institutionalization of intellectual work has a significant

---

[30] Eyerman (1994), p. 191.

impact on the way that ideas interact with society. As professionals and experts, even as academic experts, intellectuals' authority rests not on the quality of their ideas, but on the claim to expertise. The language they speak becomes increasingly technical and specialized, and not a vernacular that can be understood by the public. The new language of the academic expert reflects a lifestyle that is devoted to a narrow specialism. Through this process, the very content of intellectual activity alters. Fridjonsdottir has drawn attention to the way that activities such as literary criticism have become almost '[an] exclusively professionalized activity of predominantly academically trained persons'. She claims that this has changed both the form and the content of this activity, so that a literary critic who fails to keep up with new fashions in cultural criticism is not likely to survive long in his or her profession.[31]

The manifest tendency towards the professionalization of intellectual life has led some writers on this subject to question the viability of the role of the independent intellectual. It is frequently suggested that the pressure of the market also directly impacts on the realm of ideas. A high level of specialization encourages knowledge to become more and more fragmented, which undermines the ability of the intellectual to engage with society as a whole. Writing in this vein, Eyerman points to the 'power of market forces to determine the content of cultural production'.[32]

There is little doubt that the power of market forces can have a significant influence over the content of cultural production. But it is not the market that has led to the retreat of the intellectual. In previous times, intellectuals thrived through reacting against the market – today, they are more likely to attempt to realize their

[31] Katrin Fridjonsdottir (1987), 'The Modern Intellectual: In Power or Disarmed? Reflections on the Sociology of Intellectuals and Intellectual Work', in Eyerman (1987), p. 121.
[32] Eyerman (1994), p. 92.

ambition through it. The idea that intellectuals have been the unwitting victims of circumstances beyond their control over-looks the fact that they have tended to embrace the opportunities offered through the institutionalization of intellectual work. Intellectuals have played a key role in promoting specialisms and academic disciplines. The idealism of the intellectual has given way to pragmatism, and a distinctly instrumentalist approach towards life.

The sense of intellectual independence has given way to a demand for institutional affirmation and recognition. This development is particularly striking in the contemporary debates that surround the absence of the public intellectual. The debate that began as an attempt to account for the decline of the independent intellectual has turned into a demand by some of its contributors that institutions and public bodies help rescue the public intellectual from extinction. Some American universities have responded to this concern as if it were a market opportunity, and have launched graduate programmes designed to train public intellectuals. Others have called upon public institutions to do more to promote the activity of the intellectual. Writing in this vein, two American academics state:

> Finally, we call for greater institutional and material recogni-tion of these multiple forms of public intellectual work. This includes both valuing and fostering public work. For example, for those who pursue service learning, institutions might provide or require training or certification, involve all faculty in some sort of service learning, and provide release time or course load reduction for those who elaborately embed themselves in community work.[33]

The demand for certifying public intellectual work indicates just how much the idea of intellectual independence has given way to

---

[33] Brouwer and Squires (2003), p. 212.

the ethos of professionalization. When intellectual identity is made contingent upon institutional approval, then it clearly ceases to have anything in common with the classical aspiration for intellectual autonomy.

It is difficult to explain the credentialist mentality of today's professional thinker as the direct consequence of the power of market forces. No doubt the expansion of the market for professionals and experts has influenced developments, but it cannot account for the readiness with which people have adopted forms of behaviour that are inconsistent with the role of the traditional intellectual. To understand why this occurred, it is necessary to look for explanations beyond the structural changes that affect the conduct of intellectual work.

The devaluation of the role of the intellectual

Although changes to the structure of society have important implications for understanding the demise of the intellectual, they do not explain why its status has become devalued. In particular, at a time when education, knowledge and intellectual labour are in such high demand, why should there be so many question marks raised over the survival of the traditional critical intellectual? Whatever the answer to this question, it is evident that most contributions on this subject have given up on the traditional critical intellectual, and are busy attempting to find a new role for the intellectual.

It is widely believed that in the so-called postmodern era, where the fundamental tenets of the Enlightenment have been called into question, the role of the critical intellectual has been severely compromised. Since many of the ideals associated with the exercise of intellectual authority – the search for knowledge, the application of reason – have become targets of scepticism, the work of the intellectual has lost some of its cultural appeal. The decline of belief in the power of reasoning has significantly weakened the status of the intellectual. An all-embracing view of the world, which was said to influence the outlook of the classical intellectual, has given way to the conviction that such a broad outlook is beyond the capacity of the human imagination.

As a result, the intellectual has been assigned a role that is far more limited than was the case in the past. Even those who retain a positive point of reference towards the critical intellectual appear to believe that it can only survive in a seriously modified form. 'While the contexts for their emergence may have been narrowed, and the range of possibilities thereby reduced, the traditions that constitute the intellectual are more than just a fading memory,' writes Eyerman. But despite the attempt to reassure that the traditions associated with the intellectual are 'more than just a fading memory', Eyerman ends up with a fairly modest and pessimistic vision of the future of intellectual work. 'Although its meaning has been almost entirely altered by what has been called the postmodern condition, the concept of the intellectual still provides a living resource which is likely to be called upon as a rallying cry for coming generations of dissidents.'[34]

The belief that the 'postmodern condition' has fundamentally transformed the terrain of intellectual activity has had a powerful impact on the way thinkers think about themselves and their activities. Unlike the Enlightenment intellectual who acclaimed the vision of universalism, today's thinkers are much more likely to celebrate a particularistic identity. Today we have English intellectuals, Black intellectuals, Feminist, Gay and Jewish intellectuals. As a result, intellectual authority does not rest on the ability to represent the truth but on the capacity to affirm the identity of a particular group or specialism. The shift from a universalist to a particularistic focus should not be seen as merely

---

[34] Eyerman (1994), pp. 199 and 200.

a variation in scale. It involves a fundamental redefinition of intellectual ambition from the attempt to go beyond particular experience to the desire to affirm it.[35] Such affirmation is dominated by an intensely conservative imperative that is hostile to the critical questioning of society.

Bauman argues that one of the consequences of post-modernity is a fundamental change in the role of the intellectual from that of a legislator to that of an interpreter. In their legislator role, intellectuals make authoritative statements that have a direct bearing on the shaping of public opinion. In their role as postmodern interpreter, intellectuals are in the business of facilitating communication – translating statements made within one communally based tradition, so that they can be understood within the system of knowledge based on another tradition.[36]

The downsizing of intellectual authority was vigorously advocated by Michel Foucault, who took the view that since there is no truly universal truth, intellectuals cannot be in the business of conveying universal truth. He claimed that thinkers could aspire to be, not universal, but 'specific' intellectuals. Specific intellectuals are not expected to make broad pronounce-ments about the problems of the world – rather they are able to devote their work to areas in which they have the most expertise, thus acquiring tangible results.

Views such as those held by Bauman and Foucault reflect the experience of demoralization with the workings of the Enlight-enment legacy. But whereas Bauman recognizes the importance for intellectuals to promote the 'process of enlightenment', Foucault is delighted with the demise of the universalist intellectual. For Foucault and others who are attracted to the outlook of postmodernism, the present era of intellectual life

[35] These points are developed in Furedi (1992), chapter 8.
[36] Bauman (1987), pp. 4–5.

actually represents a major advance over the past.[37] The reigning
in of intellectual energy is often depicted as a responsible and
pragmatic accommodation to the demands of postmodern times,
and there is a palpable sense of satisfaction with compromise
among the new breed of postmodernist conformist intellectuals.

The conformist intellectual

Intellectuals in the past were often concerned about attempts to
undermine the pursuit of their activities. Political intervention
directed at intellectual autonomy and the commercial pressures of
the market were often criticized by the radical intelligentsia.
Today, radical voices are less inclined to be concerned about
attacks on free speech, censorship and the battle for ideas.
Whereas criticism of the traditional critical intellectual was
previously voiced mainly by the polemicists of the political right,
today it is far more likely to be articulated by the left. So the
introduction to a recently published collection of essays on the
subject of the intellectual by a leftist academic, patronizingly
dismisses the 'older and less morally creditable conception of
intellectuals'.[38]

In previous times, radical intellectuals often confronted the
upholders of tradition to demand change and the transformation
of cultural life. That is why the most strident anti-intellectual
voices tended to be the upholders of tradition. Today, it is no
longer the representatives of cultural conservatism who celebrate
and seek to defend the status quo. On the contrary, intellectuals

---

[37] Since postmodernists tend to eschew definitions, postmodern is a fluid and
confusing concept that is difficult to define. Postmodernists are hostile to
the idea that truth can be objective, are sceptical of the authority of science
and resist the idea of progress.

[38] See Bruce Robbins, 'Introduction: The grounding of Intellectuals', in
Robbins (1990), p. xiv.

of the right are often appalled by cultural life and would like to see fundamental institutional and cultural changes. The defence of cultural and educational institutions, which is traditionally assumed by the political right, has been adopted by professionals and experts involved in intellectual work.

A profound mood of new conservatism shapes deliberations on the role of the intellectual. There has never been a period since the beginning of modernity when people working with ideas were so complacent about their role. This atmosphere of conformism is particularly evident among professional academics. Any suggestion that intellectual life faces exhaustion, or is in any sense inferior to what existed in previous times, is perfunctorily dismissed as a despicable attempt to return to some elitist inspired mythical age. According to one such account, 'for intellectuals, there is certainly no need to despair', since 'the life that goes on in the university, the pedagogy we conduct amid the ruins, is different from, livelier and more rigorous than, what the various legends of the truth's decline and the intellectual's demise have led us to believe'. The author of these words even has a few crumbs of comfort to offer to those concerned with the marginalization of the Enlightenment tradition. 'For those who get it, the values of the Enlightenment still furnish the patches of brightness by which we choose our way,' he writes.[39] Finding 'patches of brightness' in order to avoid engaging with the retreat of the intellectual seems to be the dominant response to the problem.

Following Foucault, many contributors are positively delighted that the Enlightenment stands are now discredited. Andrew Ross is pleased that the agenda is no longer dominated by a universalist outlook. For Ross, 'the withering away of the universal intellectual' represents a positive step forward. He reserves his scorn for those who still yearn for the intellectual culture of a previous era, and denounces what he calls the

[39] Michael (2000), pp. 174–5.

'reactionary consensus of left and right, each unswervingly loyal to their respective narratives of decline'. Ross dismisses charges of 'post-sixties fragmentation and academification from unreconstructed voices on the left, and warnings of doom and moral degeneracy from the Cassandras on the right'.[40] In this view, all is well – the only flies in the ointment are the twisted critics of the professionalization of academic life.

The assumption that classical intellectual authority is no longer sustainable informs today's conformist cultural outlook. 'For those who take seriously the diagnosis that public life in Western democracies is no longer of a kind that permits claims to general intellectual authority, declinism, of whatever political coloring, is too plainly a posture rather than an answer', argues the editor of a collection of articles on 'The Public Intellectual'.[41] Serious concern with the malaise of intellectual life often invites the smug response that all is well in academia. The questioning of contemporary intellectual and pedagogic practices is frequently dismissed as a lament for a golden age. This complacent defence of the status quo is virtually unprecedented in the intellectual history of modernity. In the nineteenth century, even the most conservative section of the intelligentsia was critical of the prevailing cultural climate, and every brand of intellectuals sought to alter, improve, transform and even overthrow the world that confronted them. The contrast between this tradition of intellectual ferment, and the complacent attitudes displayed today, highlights the distinct features of intellectual life in the early twenty-first century.

One of the most systematic endorsements of intellectual conformism is presented in the writings of Bruce Robbins, professor of English at Rutgers University. Robbins appears as a wholehearted supporter of academic professionalism because he believes that it has created an environment hospitable to new

---

[40]   Ross (1989), pp. 211 and 229.
[41]   Small (2002), p. 5.

minority voices.[42] Robbins embraces academic professionalism on account of the fact that that the cultural left has thrived and benefited in this environment. 'Thanks to the Reaganite backlash, much of the public has thus learned that, for better or worse, the left has a powerful presence in American cultural life,' he brags. Robbins also boasts of the left's own 'cultural and institutional achievements' and writes of the 'grounding of intellectuals' in universities.[43] Robbins does not merely applaud the success of the left in 'grounding itself within American educational and cultural institutions since the 1960s' – he self-consciously deprecates the legacy of the 'old' intellectuals and their 'abysmal record' of behaviour.[44]

Although Robbins continually alludes to the supposed triumph of the cultural left, what he is really describing is the displacement of the vocation of the intellectual by the academic professional. His lack of concern with the erosion of the independence and autonomy of the intellectual is matched by a pragmatic adaptation to the demands of academic institutionalism. From this standpoint, the devaluation of the role of intellectual autonomy is represented as a positive blow against old-fashioned elitism. The new intellectual gains authority from his institution, and does not require a sense of autonomy. Of course not every academic acquiesces to the institutionalization of intellectual life and adopts the conformist identity of a housekept thinker. And many institutionalized intellectuals yearn to achieve a degree of autonomy from institutional pressures. Most academics tend to be intelligent professionals and astute experts, who sadly are not culturally equipped to play the role of the public intellectual. They belong to their institutions and remain estranged from the world of the public.

---

[42] Robbins (1993), chapter 1.
[43] See Bruce Robbins, 'Introduction: The Grounding of Intellectuals', in Robbins (1990), pp. x and xi.
[44] See Bruce Robbins, 'Introduction: The Grounding of Intellectuals' in Robbins (1990), p. xiii.

2   Trivial Pursuits

Contemporary Western society has a love–hate relationship with knowledge. On one hand we pursue it and celebrate it, employing people to gain knowledge of market conditions, the mood of the nation or what makes your three-year-old child tick. Since September 11, opinion-makers have often complained that we simply do not know enough about why terrorism has become such a global threat or why Muslim societies appear to resent the West. It seems that we don't have enough people with a colloquial knowledge of Middle East languages. To put it crudely, we are worried about our lack of knowledge and fear that we may be deficient in intelligence about what is going on in large chunks of the world. We take Knowledge very, very seriously, as expressions like 'knowledge is power' only confirm.

At the same time, however, society is uncomfortable with the pursuit of knowledge, and often distrustful of those who claim to know. There is widespread suspicion of scientific authority, and people who attempt to extend the boundaries of scientific knowledge find themselves accused of 'playing God'. Such accusations are not only levelled at individuals involved in controversial areas like genetic research or nanotechnology, but also at those who attempt to gain a better understanding of human health in general. Social scientists who seek knowledge with a capital K are disparaged for their attachment to 'meta-narratives' with the same intensity that is generally directed at genetic research. In the past, it was often said that a 'little knowledge is a dangerous thing'. Today, society is confronted with a strong undercurrent of opinion that suggests that 'too much knowledge threatens human survival'.

The co-existence of an insatiable appetite for more knowledge and an intense suspicion of its further development is one of the paradoxes of Western culture today. The constant demand for scientific evidence exists alongside apprehensions about what the scientist is up to in the laboratory. The massive investment in education, universities and private research has not led to the flourishing of a public scientific, cultural or intellectual discourse. The younger generations appear to be turned off by mathematics and science, and it is not intellectual curiosity but hostility and suspicion that animates the debates on these subjects. Nor has public reaction against experimentation and progress led to the establishment of alternative outlets for the development of intellectual curiosity. In previous times, when young people became estranged from science they turned to the humanities and liberal arts. Today's generation of students has adopted a distinctly pragmatic approach, and is as turned off by history, social theory and philosophy as it is by science. In the US, between 1970 and 1995, the number of history majors graduated by American colleges and universities decreased by 39 per cent, foreign language majors declined by 37 per cent, and English departments lost 10 per cent of their students.[1] And this decline occurred at a time when the numbers attending colleges has increased at a steady rate! The public's unease towards existing scientific knowledge is complemented by a tangible sense of indifference towards its further development.

The public's unease with the development of knowledge does not, however, mean that it has ceased to be curious about how the world works. There is an enormous public appetite for popular science books. Historical biographies often make the

---

[1]   Russell Berman and Stephen Haber, 'Whatever Happened to the Academic Left?', *Hoover Digest*, 2002, no. 2.

bestseller lists, while television programmes devoted to historical and scientific themes can always secure a substantial audience of curious individuals. Many people really want to learn about the world. But in a world where the pursuit of knowledge lacks powerful cultural affirmation, people's relation to it acquires a passive character. Yes, people buy popular science books but they rarely get together to discuss and debate the issues they contain. Many individuals have sought to exploit the opportunities provided by the Internet to pursue their ideas or to learn about subjects that interest them. But this welcome development is driven as much by suspicion of official sources of knowledge as it is by the impulse for exploring new ideas.

Society's uneasy relationship to knowledge is influenced by the same forces that are responsible for the changing status of the intellectual. The authoritative status that modernity has tradi-tionally assigned to knowledge has come under challenge from a variety of sources: disappointment with the promise of the Enlightenment and Modernity; a sense of powerlessness regard-ing our ability to know the future; the consequent growth in the influence of a relativist approach towards knowledge; and the replacement of the pursuit of Knowledge with a pragmatic focus on specialist micro-knowledges.

Disenchantment with the Enlightenment tradition

From its conception, the Enlightenment was subject to hostility and criticism. Opponents of the Enlightenment were bitterly suspicious of the claim that the human capacity to reason could ensure steady progress and improve the condition of life. From the outset, advocates of the Enlightenment were accused of playing God. The optimistic humanist celebration of the capacity to know was dismissed by religious and conservative philosophers as a malevolent project designed to undermine the realm of the sacred. Opponents of the Enlightenment believed that rationality undermined the spiritual connections that linked people to God, to their traditions and communities. It was felt that any strategy to achieve rational change must upset the existing precarious balance and inevitably make things worse.

Rationalism was also decried, because it was felt to be antithetical to the flourishing of the human soul. Anti-Enlightenment critics claimed that the privileged status assigned to reason marginalized the spiritual and moral dimension of life. The promotion of reason and scientific knowledge was held responsible for the decline of religion and consequently the creation of a spiritual or emotional vacuum. It was even suggested that the loss of previously held spiritual certainties was responsible for the growth of fanaticism and totalitarianism. According to Conor Cruise O'Brien, the Enlightenment created an 'emotional vacuum' which was filled by nationalism. The bitter Europe-wide war that ensued is therefore represented as an indirect legacy of the Enlightenment, and before even a plea for mitigation can be entered, he insists that 'the responsibility, though indirect, was real, through the creation of that cosmic emotional vacuum'.[2]

Anxiety towards the pursuit of knowledge and reason was motivated by the conviction that it would disrupt the precarious balance that existed between different groups in society. Anti-Enlightenment thinkers genuinely believed that knowledge was dangerous because it threatened to weaken the faith and beliefs that helped keep the otherwise irrational masses from disrupting society. It was felt that too much education and knowledge would contribute to an explosion of instability, since what held the masses in check was religion and deference to authority. That is

2   C. Cruise O'Brien, 'Paradise Lost', in *New York Review of Books*, 25 April 1991, p. 58.

why many upholders of tradition feared the advance of reason. As the conservative philosopher Joseph de Maistre explained:

> Man's cradle must be surrounded by dogmas and when his reason awakens, he must find all his opinions already made, at least those concerning his social behaviour. Nothing is more important for man than prejudice.[3]

In this anti-modernist imagination, prejudice and dogma were directly linked to the enforcement of order and the maintenance of cohesion. By contrast, knowledge and reason were greeted as the harbingers of uncertainty, confusion and instability.

It is important to recall that the anti-Enlightenment reaction of the nineteenth century remained subordinate to the prevailing sense of dynamism and progress. Overall, public enthusiasm for science, and a general belief in the power of reason and progress, encouraged a positive cultural valuation of knowledge. In such circumstances experimentation, change and even revolution were often interpreted as symptoms of historical progress. As William Wordsworth wrote in celebration of the French Revolution:

> Bliss was it in that dawn to be alive
> To be young was very heaven

Today Wordsworth's sentiments appear incongruent with social attitudes towards change. The fear of change filters into every aspect of social thought. The pervasive existence of this sentiment has been underwritten by the overwhelming image of failure associated with past attempts at social transformation. The conclusion drawn by most commentaries is that the attempt to change society leads to a situation that is actually worse than what existed previously. It is claimed that the attempt to pursue public policies wedded to rationalism have in fact made the situation far worse. Knowledge, ideas and especially ideologies

---

[3]   Cited in Giner (1976), p. 40.

linked to the Enlightenment, are denounced on the grounds that they bear responsibility for much of the destruction inflicted on people in the twentieth century. One British political columnist has argued that 'transformational ideologies have inflicted vast harm upon our century and a death toll numbering many millions'.[4] This observation resonates with the widely held disenchantment with the legacy of the Enlightenment.

The tendency to limit the application of reason has become a dominant feature of Western intellectual life. In a recent survey of this subject, the well-known American sociologist Jeffrey Alexander wrote about the 'omnipresence of irrationality'. According to Alexander, reason 'has been experienced as a hollow shell, progress as inconceivable, and often actually undesirable'.[5] Even proponents of the Enlightenment find it difficult to promote a robust view of the world that is embedded in the values of reason and progress. The best-case scenario that Morris Berman's *The Twilight of American Culture* is able to posit is one where 'we do have renaissance, a preservation and transmission of Enlightenment culture but only for a select few, and their impact on the rest of culture is apparently nonexistent'.[6] The reaction against reason today is far stronger than at any time since the development of capitalism. In the nineteenth century, the romantic revolt against reason did not question the possibility of knowing: it merely challenged one possible – that is, the rational – form of knowing. Today, the very possibility of knowing has been called into question by people who claim that the world has become far too complex to understand.

The reaction against the Enlightenment can also be understood as a rejection of the authority of knowledge. The argument that human knowledge is limited is consistently used

[4]   Peter Jenkins, 'New Dreams of Liberty', in *Independent*, 14 May 1991.
[5]   Alexander, 'Between progress ...', in Alexander and Sztompka (1990), p. 26.
[6]   Berman (2001).

to discredit attempts to improve social circumstances through public policy or scientific advance. The depreciation of reason and understanding justifies the politics of scepticism towards intellectual authority, science and Knowledge. In previous decades, this attitude was most vigorously promoted by individuals on the right wing of the political spectrum. Irrationalist thinkers of the nineteenth century, such as Nietzsche and Schopenhauer, argued that it is ignorance rather than knowledge that characterizes the human condition. Theirs was a history where chaos and chance are far more significant than meaning. Unease with the potential for reasoning was also evident among many of the founders and leading lights of the new social sciences. Max Weber, who remains to this day one of the most influential sociologists, believed that there were important limits to the application of reason. He took the view that reason had little relevance for understanding values. In contrast to the permanence of art, Weber regarded science as having only a transient existence. 'In science, each of us knows that what he has accomplished will be antiquated in ten, twenty, fifty years', he wrote.[7] The restricted role that Weber assigned to reasoning was motivated by his doubts about the possibility of knowing. Today, the dominant critique of rationality is more likely to be influenced by the *fear* of knowledge. There is an influential body of thought that claims that Enlightenment rationality has been responsible for some of the most destructive episodes of human history, while the experience of modernity is often dismissed as a destructive one that logically culminated in the Holocaust. According to one account, the attempt to exterminate Jewish people was an 'exercise in the rational management of society'.[8] This thesis posits the 'promotion of rationality' as a heartless amoral cause that is indifferent to the

---

[7] Cited in Furedi (1992), p. 206.
[8] Bauman (1991), p. 72.

sanctity of life, and therefore possesses a capacity for 'generating the Holocaust-like solution'.[9]

Today, the most bitter denunciations of the Enlightenment come, not from the right, but from radical voices who believe that the very pursuit of knowledge through science, technology and innovation threatens the world. They point to tragic events like the Holocaust as proof of the threat represented by the single-minded pursuit of rationality and knowledge. The far more plausible idea that associates the Holocaust with the triumph of irrationality and the failure to develop the potential of the Enlightenment tradition is sadly overlooked. Instead, the potential for unleashing the power of destruction overwhelms the contemporary imagination. It is the destructive, not the creative, potential of knowledge that shapes today's public imagination.

A sense of powerlessness in the face of uncertainty

Disappointment with the promise of the Enlightenment has diminished public confidence in society's ability to know, understand and ultimately control the future. The view that we live in a world that is so complex as to render meaningless the claim to know is systematically promoted by radical critics of modernity. Critics are also worried that the advance of knowledge itself creates problems, because it threatens to encourage activity and behaviour whose consequences cannot be known in advance. This attitude is most forcefully expressed in the view that one of the products of science and knowledge is risk.

Leading sociologists Ulrich Beck and Anthony Giddens forcefully argue the case for the close association between the sense of risk and the increase of knowledge. 'Many of the

---

[9]   Bauman (1991), pp. 28 and 29.

uncertainties which face us today have been created by the very
growth of knowledge', wrote Giddens, and Beck has noted that
the 'sources of danger are no longer ignorance but knowledge'.[10]
In this scenario, knowledge through its application creates both
new hazards and an awareness of their risk. The claim that the
problem is not ignorance but knowledge fundamentally questions
the authority of science. The implicit preference of ignorance over
knowledge represents a contemporary variant of the conservative
embrace of prejudice in the nineteenth century. In both cases,
knowledge is perceived as undesirable because of its disruptive
and disorienting effect.

The association of knowledge with risk is based on a model of
society that is uncomfortable with change and uncertainty, and
feels continually under threat from technological development.
Such a society experiences the advance of knowledge and the
unintended consequences of technological development as a
source of anxiety and disorientation. These days, arguments that
associate knowledge with risks are implicitly questioning the
human potential for knowing. It is claimed that human knowledge cannot grasp the chaotic patterns of events set in motion by
global capitalism, and the impossibility of knowing or calculating
the consequences of technology and human action is widely
insisted upon. This view is justified by the argument that
technological development in a globalized environment has
become so complex as to destroy the foundation for understanding the future. As a result, the German sociologist Nikolas
Luhmann claims that 'no one is in a position to claim knowledge
of the future nor the capacity to change it'.[11] For Luhmann,
knowledge is restricted to providing insights about what has
already happened, and rather limited insights at that.

---

[10] A. Giddens, 'Risk, Trust, Reflexivity', in Beck et al. (1994), p. 85 and Beck
      (1992), p. 183.
[11] Luhman (1993), p. 48.

Frequently, risk is conceptualized in relation to our inability to know. Often what is at issue is not just not-knowing but the impossibility of knowing. The association of knowledge with potential danger is based on a profoundly anti-humanist intellectual outlook. In this model, knowledge and science are both limited in their grasp of the truth; and because they set in motion innovations that have unintended effects, they also create problems. Such an outlook is, of course, strongly shaped by the negative experience of political change in the twentieth century. The failure of political experimentation in the Soviet Union and China, disappointment with the record of the Welfare State and disenchantment with the promise of the Enlightenment is interpreted as direct proof that ambitious political programmes do not work; and, retrospectively, such negative experiences confirm that we simply do not know how to know. Thus, the authority of knowledge is further devalued.

The preoccupation with uncertainty and risk does not explicitly lead to the rejection of knowledge. Rather, it helps to consolidate a mood that assigns to knowledge an essentially defensive role. From this precautionary perspective, knowledge is required to accommodate to the prevailing climate of uncertainty and anxiety. The sense of powerlessness with which change is perceived has weakened people's belief in the possibility of knowing what lies ahead, reflected in the demand that 'science must not run ahead of public opinion', and the notion that the ethos of precaution must dictate the pace at which knowledge develops. The development of knowledge has always been subject to pragmatic concerns, but today such concerns have a distinctly defensive focus. And because the authority of knowledge has been compromised through experience, the argument that it should be allowed to be pursued for its own sake carries less conviction then in previous times.

Relativism: the contestation of knowledge claims

The sense of powerlessness in the face of uncertainty is reinforced by the sentiment that meaning and truth elude our grasp. In turn, the disorientation and anxiety bred by uncertainty has helped foster a mood that is hospitable to the ceaseless questioning of knowledge and truth. Such reactions readily converge with the anti-Enlightenment disdain for the idea of universalistic truths. In the nineteenth century, the project of relativizing knowledge was designed to shield tradition against the claims of universalism. Cultural relativism sought to protect religion and traditional morality and values against what was perceived as the threat posed by science, objective truths and universal values. According to opponents of the Enlightenment, different communities had a particular way of making sense of the world, and their values were the product of their own specific circumstances. It was claimed that each of these particular perspectives was of equal validity and provided far more insight into the ways of the world than the so-called abstract universalism of the Enlightenment.

Since the 1960s, cultural relativism has succeeded in becoming a powerful intellectual force. Disenchantment with the Enlightenment tradition has encouraged many thinkers and sections of the public to make sense of their lives through particularistic perspectives. The caricatured version of universalism upheld by the institutions of Western society proved to be no match to the powerful spirit of disenchantment that prevailed in the second half of the twentieth century.[12] One consequence of this process was to put the authority of objective truth on the defensive – and thereby putting to question all truth claims.

Whereas in the past the most systematic critique of universalism was mounted by the right, today, by contrast, the

---

[12] This argument is developed at length in Furedi (1992).

cultural left is its most aggressive opponent. Since the late eighteenth century, concepts such as reason, progress and universalism have been generally associated with the left. But, since the 1960s, the New Left has begun a systematic demolition of those values, by questioning the claims of reason, progress and universalism. The new philosophical posture was reflected in the political approach that acclaimed diversity and opposed uni-versalistic values.[13] Unlike the nineteenth-century critics of the Enlightenment, the New Left was not, in its origin, motivated by a conservative impulse to defend tradition. But because Western capitalism presented its values as universal, the New Left unthinkingly became opposed to it. The New Left not only rejected universalism in general, it adopted a particularistic world-view linked to the politics of identity. Unconsciously, the New Left reaction to postwar Western capitalism internalized the methods and arguments of the conservative reaction to the Enlightenment.

During the 1960s, the left's love affair with relativism was hesitant and semi-conscious, but by the late 1970s, radical intellectuals and, more often, ex-radicals were speaking the language of Nietzsche. In a process aptly described by Alan Bloom as the 'Nietzscheanization of the Left', the left, repelled by modernism, took a cultural turn towards particularism, hetero-geneity and difference. It is worth recalling that the original methodological orientation towards difference began as the defence of aristocratic and ruling-class privilege. Differences in moral and mental capacities were advanced to account for and legitimize the social hierarchy. By the mid-nineteenth century, this perspective attached itself to racial differences and helped to legitimize the notion that there was a global hierarchy of people. The cultural left did not set out, as the Social Darwinist did, to provide intellectual sustenance to racial superiority. But the

[13] For a discussion of this development, see Furedi (1992), chapter 8.

conservative potential of a particularistic doctrine has crystallized into the cultural left's suspicion of cosmopolitan and global trends. As the rebellion against the rhetoric of universalism turned into a celebration of difference, the process of intellectual de-radicalization became inescapable. The outcome has been the ascendancy of what is called postmodernism and its systematic repudiation of objective knowledge.

Today's postmodernists follow the path set out by the anti-Enlightenment reaction of the nineteenth century. They claim that all knowledge is socially constructed; therefore, all knowledges are incommensurable and all knowledges are in principle, equally valid. Truth depends entirely on the perspective adopted. Postmodernists frequently claim that there is no single road to understanding. This insistence on difference also pertains to methodology – truths are arrived at by different methods. The elaboration of the relativization of methodology is one of the distinctive characteristics of postmodernism. It is based on the old romantic conviction that the road to understanding is through subjectivity, specifically intuition. Postmodernists have elaborated this idea to suggest that since there are many truths, there are also many valid ways of getting there. It is also suggested that those who live a particular experience are best capable of understanding it. Some would claim they are the *only* ones fit to comment on their particular experience.

The elaboration of methodological relativism is rarely made explicit. In general, it assumes the polemical form of an accusation of cultural imperialism or ethnocentrism. For example, in the United States it has been strongly suggested that only blacks have the right to write black history. During the past three decades a number of groups have taken out a patent on their soul, and their unique way of knowing becomes the validation of their knowledge. Of all groups, academic feminism has the most elaborated particularistic epistemology. In reaction to an apparently male-centred world-view, some cultural feminists try to project a female-centred one. Carole Gilligan's *A Woman's Way of Knowing* clearly expresses the trend towards the marriage of subjective experience and knowledge. Moreover, as Novick writes, 'for many feminists the ideology of "difference" extended to fundamental questions of cognitive style and epistemological values'.[14]

Specific female qualities are abstracted by feminist theorists to elaborate women's perspective. Needless to say, from this exclusivist cultural point of view only women can know women. Novick reminds us that by the 'late 1970s the assertion that women's history could only be legitimately written from a feminist standpoint was no longer argued; it was a settled question, beyond argument'.[15]

The denunciation of 'Western rationality' or 'male logic' assumes that theorizing and knowing is to be equated with experiencing. This perspective contends that the path to the truth is above all through subjective experience rather than theorizing or contemplating. Yet being black or white or male or female or disabled or Japanese does not confer a privileged access to the knowledge of the experience. As Mattick persuasively argues, being part of a culture does not give the individual greater understanding of that culture than those who study it from the outside. He writes that 'participants in a culture, even while they may (and indeed must) know the rules and criteria regulating social behaviour in that culture, may have only a very vague notion of how the parts of social life in which they participate fit together'. To strengthen his point, Mattick cites Fritz Machlup's illustration of an alien Martian anthropologist who observes the stock market and interviews its participants:

> Since probably 999 out of 1000 persons on the stock market do
> not really know what it does and how it does it, the most

[14] See Novick (1988), p. 494.
[15] See Novick (1988), p. 496.

diligent observer-plus-interviewer would remain largely ignor-
ant. Alas, economics cannot be learned either by watching or
by interviewing the people engaged in economic activities. It
takes a good deal of theorizing before one can grasp the
complex interrelations in an economic system.[16]

Observation, like experience, is meaningless outside the frame-
work of a theory. The precondition for a sound account of how
the stock exchange works is not contingent on being employed
there. Someone with the possession of a sound theory of
economic life is far more likely to grasp the intricate workings
of the stock market.

The tendency to equate knowledge with the insights that
people gain from fragmentary experience makes it impossible to
have a meaningful common standard to evaluate knowledge
claims. Through transforming knowledge into knowledges, the
role of the intellectual has become compromised. The knowledge
possessed by the intellectual can be interpreted as just a point of
view with no special significance for society. It is not only the role
of the intellectual that has been affected by this trend. The
growing trend towards the relativization of knowledge claims has
had a significant impact on pedagogic theories and practice.
Many educationalists now regard experiential learning as having
a status comparable to theoretical knowledge

The doctrine of cultural relativism has contributed to the
flourishing of pedagogic theories that encourage a philistine
attitude towards knowledge. Today, the postmodern influence on
education theory has become widespread. Its suspicion towards
universal standards is recycled in schools through criticizing
systems of assessment based on a common standard. Some
postmodern educationalists argue that knowledge itself –
rationality and objectivity is merely a male prejudice. Dale

---

[16] Mattick (1986), p. 32.

Spender and Elizabeth Sarah argue that male experts have constructed 'educational knowledge' so as to control who passes and who fails. In place of 'educational knowledge', these influential critics call for the recognition of 'personal knowledge'. They argue that 'everyone has a personal knowledge which is valid and there is no way of classifying this'.[17] In schools, the subjective experience of children has been endowed with considerable authority. From this perspective, the role assigned to teachers is not to teach knowledge that is external to this experience, but to cultivate and bring out insights that the child already possesses. As one critic of this development argues: 'the redefinition of knowledge as the subjective experience of the child has entailed a shift in emphasis from teacher to learner'.[18] The celebration of children's particular experience is systematically pursued in school textbooks, which are dominated by the ethos of relevance. It appears that children must not be confronted with images and ideas that are alien to their experience. In subjects like history and literature, classical stories are helpfully 'updated' in order to help children understand them.

But what exactly is personal knowledge? It is what children learn through their personal experience. For children, personal knowledge is what they learn at home, from their peers and from the media. Such personal knowledge provides children with valuable insights about the world but does not provide them with the education that enables them to question, conceptualize, problem-solve and to develop intellectually. The equation of 'personal knowledge 'with 'educational knowledge' fails to distinguish between the arbitrary experience of a child and the systematic attempt to develop his or her potential.

But it is in the university system where the line that divides knowledge from everyday insight has become most blurred.

---

[17] Spender and Sarah (1992), p. 42.
[18] Phillips (1998), pp. 48–9.

Advocates of wider participation often attempt to weaken the authority of intellectual knowledge in order to facilitate access to higher education. This approach is justified on the grounds that it is a student-based, rather than a subject-based, approach to learning. One of the ways that advocates of this policy seek to realize their objective is through the accreditation of prior learning, where students are effectively rewarded for learning about their experiences of life before arriving at university. From this perspective, the insights gained through the banal routine of daily existence are qualitatively similar to the knowledge gained through systematic study.

Support for recognizing 'personal knowledge' is not confined to postmodernist theorists. The government exam boards and many universities all now accept accreditation of prior knowledge as a useful assessment tool. Personal experience is given academic credence and homemakers are accepted on courses because their life experiences of budget planning, organizational skills and communicating are represented as the equivalent of a Communication Studies A level. One advocate of accrediting prior learning explains the approach in the following terms:

> The justification normally given for thus using experiential learning is based on the assumption that people have learnt and continue to learn through their life and work experience. They bring this learning with them to higher education and therefore it can be recognized through appropriate assessment. This involves systematizing it in terms of specific knowledge and skills, a process that is thought to require reflection. In effect the raw material of subjective experience is transformed into 'objective' statements of learning outcomes.[19]

Lessons learnt through the school of life are recycled as

---

[19]   Robin Usher, 'Qualification, Paradigms and Experimental Learning in Higher Education', in Fulton (1989), p. 65.

knowledge through the administrative process of subjecting them to learning outcomes. If this process simply involved another small dose of credentialism, there would be little need to remark on it. But the very process of assigning authority to prior learning devalues the authority of real knowledge. The lessons of life may be interesting and pertinent to the individual concerned but, even at their best, reflections on individual experience are far too arbitrary, specific and personal to generate knowledge that can give meaning and understanding to people in society. Knowledge is often produced through detaching people from their immediate experience, so that they can transcend their specific circumstances and through their position of detachment learn to appropriate the insights generated by society as a whole.

The devaluation of the authority of knowledge is not an accidental side effect of the crusade to accredit prior learning. Those who support the cause of the 'access movement' do not hold in high regard the knowledge gained through systematic study, research and experimentation. They believe not only that this knowledge is just a social construction, but that it is used to reinforce elitist privilege. This view is particularly hostile to the authority of pure research, since 'it occupies a privileged position and is an important determinant of status, the distribution of resources and general attitudes and orientations'. In addition it 'contributes to exclusivity on the grounds of the need to maintain the highest "standards" of research and relegates student-centred provision to a lower priority'.[20] Since the product of pure research is not easily accessible to most people, those who embrace the dogma of access regard it merely as an elitist obstacle that stands in the way of the realization of their cause. That is why they can so readily dismiss the hard-earned intellectual achievements of human civilization and why they

[20] Robin Usher, 'Qualification, Paradigms and Experiential Learning in Higher Education', in Fulton (1989), p. 75.

continually scorn 'standards' as something of an elitist confidence trick.

The higher education establishment has accepted the restricted status assigned to intellectual knowledge. It has done so through treating as knowledge every outcome of a learning experience. Academia has accepted that subjective emotional insights and skills-based training should be labelled 'knowledges', while accreditation of prior learning puts life skills on a par with academic qualifications, and work-related training and vocationalism on a par with scholarship. As Ron Barnett argues in his book *Realizing the University*, 'process knowledge, tacit knowledge, action learning, experiential learning: all these terms point to the multiplication of our ways of knowing in the modern world'. The multiplication of different ways of knowing deprives intellectual knowledge of any unique significance. Why bother to work hard to learn, when you can pick up a bit of experiential learning in the bar and gain formal accreditation for it?

The student-centred perspective, like other forms of the relativist world-view, continually attempts to confine knowledge to that which emerges from a particular experience. Its hostility to intellectual knowledge that transcends particularity is fuelled by the realization that its own status and authority depends on discrediting knowledge with a capital K. Its success is shown by the influence it has gained over the education establishment and its institutions. In or out of these institutions, objective knowledge does not enjoy a powerful cultural validation.

Instrumentalist compromise

Despite the intensification of trends that attempt to restrain the authority of knowledge, society continues to need insights in order to deal with the complex problems thrown up in our uncertain world. The culture of fear that influences the public's apprehension of technological innovation and experimentation coexists with the demand for more science and more knowledge of the workings of the natural world. Similarly, cultural relativism may thrive on campuses and in the arts and the media, but government and business are continually looking for objective knowledge to settle many of the disputes facing society. Pragmatism and the pressure to compete and solve new challenges ensures that there is a thriving market for objective knowledge.

Cardinal Newman, in his nineteenth-century classic defence of the liberal university, *The Idea of a University*, observed that 'Knowledge is capable of being its own end'. This idea of knowledge for its own end has seldom been realized in practice. Universities and other institutions have always been forced to engage with the pressures of conflicting interests and practical matters. Although there is a relationship of tension, the valuing of knowledge and being interested in its application can live alongside one another. Pure and applied research, and abstract and empirical theory, can thrive so long as the authority of knowledge is accepted in society. The problem today is not the pragmatic demand for practical knowledge. It is that instrumentalist pressures on knowledge production are rarely contained by a wider quest for understanding.

Instrumentalist pressure on knowledge production happily coexists with the regressive trends discussed above. Private business, government, the media and the university have internalized the mood of scepticism towards the legacy of the enlightenment. They have assimilated the precautionary attitude towards the development of knowledge and given way to the influence of relativism, especially upon culture and politics. An informal compromise has been established whereby knowledge can develop where it is practically necessary. This has led to the emergence of an uneasy coexistence of competing knowledge claims. As a result, producers of knowledge need to share cultural authority with groups who are in the business of restraining the development of reason and science.

Of course people still contribute to the development of knowledge. But in a world where knowledge production is entirely driven by pragmatic concerns, we have become devoid of the ability to decide collectively how to value and how to affirm knowledge. Without meaning, knowledge becomes less the property of the public than of the specialist, the disciplinarian and the expert. The fragmentation of intellectual life leading to the proliferation of specialisms is not simply a response to the need to engage with a complex world. The growth of specialization is fuelled by a culture where intellectuals are discouraged from looking at the big picture, and encouraged to find meaning in their specialty. Discussions are increasingly self-referential and not designed to communicate and engage people outside a specific field of speciality. In such circumstances, objective knowledge appears to have a technical character, and experts and technicians displace those searching for more profound insights. Instead of Knowledge we have developed the tendency to develop micro-knowledge.

One problem with the new group of experts, specialists and knowledge brokers is that their insights are limited to their speciality. Moreover there is no cultural support for the project of transforming those insights into a wider public discourse. Yet reality is multidimensional, and its knowledge demands that we can talk and work across disciplines and specialisms. Unfortunately even in the university, the imperative of specialization mitigates against the acquisition of the general knowledge that is a prerequisite for the functioning of a genuinely knowledge-oriented society. Ultimately the erosion of knowledge with a capital K serves to deprive society of a wider web of common meaning.

The strong cultural pressures that have promoted the feeble version of knowledge that prevails today encourage a philistine attitude towards the life of the mind. Pragmatism towards the use of knowledge can limit the damage caused by the trends discussed above. But pragmatism itself diverts intellectual energies away from realizing the potential for making a significant impact on public life, towards an obsession with narrow specialization.

3 Dumbing Down

The devaluation of the status of the intellectual and the authority of knowledge has important implications for the conduct of public life. Intellectuals in the early twenty-first century have a modest input into public debate, and the public is certainly not preoccupied with a battle of ideas. Moreover, the subordination of knowledge to pragmatic objectives has helped foster an intellectual mood that is inhospitable to experimentation and the development of powerful ideas. The displacement of the thinker by the expert has also weakened the public's interest in debating big issues. In this climate intellectuals find it difficult both to find their voice and to find an audience. As Pierre Hassner remarked, 'in the West, as in the East, not only do public intellectuals find it hard to get a hearing, but it is not certain that they have something to say'.[1]

Philistinism in the domain of culture has been paralleled by similar trends influencing public debate and political life. One of the clearest manifestations of this process is the manifest decline in the standards of political debate. Spoon-feeding the public with sound bites has become a highly prized political skill. Professional speech-writers pursue their task as if their audience was composed of easily distracted children and, not surprisingly, political discussion tends to be shallow, short-termist and bereft of ideas. This is the age of 'micro-politics', where, in Britain at

---

[1] Pierre Hassner, 'The Public Intellectual and the Experience of Totalitarianism', in Melzer *et al.* (2003), p. 138.

least, politics presents itself through the depoliticized language of managerialism, technocracy and business. Politicians promise to 'deliver', and claim that their policies add 'value' or are 'value for money'. Policies are no longer good – they are 'evidence-based'. Policies are rarely generated by a world-view – they are derived from 'best practice'. New Labour's Third Way-speak is entirely devoted to managerial process talk that promises 'transparency' and 'accountability'.

In the United States, the level of political rhetoric is indeed designed for adults who are seen to have the mental capacity of children. A disturbing study of presidential debates carried out by *The Princeton Review* analysed transcripts of the Gore–Bush debates, the Clinton–Bush–Perot debate of 1992, the Kennedy–Nixon debate of 1960, and the Lincoln–Douglas debate of 1858. It reviewed these transcripts using a standard vocabulary test that indicates the minimum educational standard needed for a reader to grasp the text. According to the analysis, during the debates of 2000, Bush spoke at a sixth-grade level (6.7) and Gore at a high seventh-grade level (7.9). In 1992, Clinton achieved a seventh-grade standard (7.6), Bush managed to achieve a sixth-grade level (6.8) as did Perot (6.3). Their contribution compares poorly with the Kennedy–Nixon exchange, where both candidates used language appropriate for tenth-graders. In turn, their achievement appears feeble compared to that of Abraham Lincoln and Stephen Douglas, whose scores were, respectively, 11.2 and 12.0.[2] No doubt sections of today's cultural elite would interpret the decline of oratory since the nineteenth century as, on balance, a positive development. In today's political rhetoric George W. Bush's sixth-grade language is obviously more 'inclusive' and less 'elitist' than that of Abraham Lincoln. But this inclusive language is symptomatic of a general tendency to treat the public as if they

---

[2]   See Diane Ravitch, 'Dumbing Down the Public: Why It Matters', in *Reason*,
      April 2001.

were not capable of understanding arguments that would test the mental capacities of a precocious ten-year-old child.

Political rhetoric in the UK is also becoming a lost art. During the 2003 party conference season, the leaders of the main parties reached a new low in the content of their speeches. Iain Duncan Smith, the leader of the Conservative Party, attempted to imitate an angry thirteen-year-old arguing with his friends in the playground. The main focus of his conference speech was repeatedly to call Tony Blair a 'liar'. For his part, Tony Blair's conference oration was so vacuous that several people who were in the audience told me that they simply could not remember what he said.

The tendency to patronize the public is sometimes presented as an attempt to connect with people who simply lack the education necessary to understand complex ideas. However, this argument fails to explain why similar trends are also evident in institutions that are devoted to the promotion of arts, culture and education. Whatever the complex reasons behind the self-conscious dumbing down of politics, its impact on the public is all too evident. A public which is continuously spoon-fed platitudes and sound bites is likely to become estranged from the world of political debate. This development is particularly striking on university campuses, where students continually insist that 'politics is boring'. The language used on campuses reflects an intense sense of cynicism towards causes and ideas, and a distinct lack of interest in holding strong views of any sort. *New York Times* journalist Michiko Kakutani's reflection on the language used by American college students captures this mood of disengagement. 'That familiar interjection "whatever" says a lot about the state of mind of college students today', notes Kakutani. He adds: 'so do the catch phrases "no problem", "not even" and "don't go there"'.[3] With such little importance attached to ideas, intel-

---

[3]   Michiko Kakutani, 'Debate? Dissent? Discussion? Oh, Don't Go There!', *New York Times*, 23 March 2002.

lectual argument has acquired negative connotations. Scholars who pursue their points with vigour can now be accused of 'academic bullying'. British universities encourage academics to ban an 'adversarial' style of debate from the seminar rooms and provide a 'supportive environment' for students. A strong argument has been redefined as a form of mental intimidation. Such attitudes are even more in evidence on American campuses. 'Debate has gotten a very bad name in our culture', notes Jeff Nunokawa, a professor of English at Princeton University. '[I]t's become synonymous with some of the most non-intellectual forms of bullying, rather than as an opportunity for deliberative democracy.'[4]

Given the extent to which the authority of knowledge has been devalued, the negative connotations acquired by conflict of opinion and heated debate are entirely understandable. With so little at stake, what's the point of arguing? If ideas have such little consequence, insistence on one's point of view appears as pig-headedness and bad manners. Criticizing someone else's ideas is readily interpreted as ego-tripping or as an act of insensitivity, while the very act of questioning someone's view can appear as a personal insult. 'It's as though there's no distinction between the person and the argument, as though to criticize an argument would be injurious to the person', observes Amanda Anderson, an English professor at Johns Hopkins University.[5] The mood of relativism, discussed in the previous chapter, reinforces the belief that insisting on the validity of an idea is a form of bad manners. If all perspectives have validity, then differences cannot be resolved through debate. 'That is your view' is the perfectly acceptable response to criticism – and a clear statement that ratifies the pointlessness of further discussion.

---

[4]   Cited in Michiko Kakutani, 'Debate? Dissent? Discussion? Oh, Don't Go There!', 23 March 2002.
[5]   Cited in Michiko Kakutani, 'Debate? Dissent? Discussion? Oh, Don't Go There!', 23 March 2002.

The powerful influence of relativist currents has made it difficult to debate matters of substance. As Russell Berman and Stephen Haber argue, 'the shared beliefs that allowed debate to take place have now largely been eroded'.[6] Without a common intellectual language and a minimalist consensus about standards, real debate becomes difficult to conduct.

The estrangement of academia from the intense and creative experience of debates that have consequences has encouraged a cultural style that celebrates intellectual disengagement. Public debate, controversy and the single-minded pursuit of ideas, once seen as fundamental features of academic life, are no longer accorded automatic respect. Academic freedom is no longer an inviolable right that people are prepared to defend. Traditionally academics, particularly social scientists, have been in the forefront of asserting the principle of freedom of speech. These days academics attempt to deny their colleagues the right to free speech. The campaign to ban Tom Paulin from speaking at Harvard for being anti-Semitic, and the censoring of Israeli academics by the editor of an academic journal based in Manchester on the grounds that they are Israeli, is a testimony to the illiberal tendencies that prevail in academia.

Academic freedom has become negotiable. In the US there has been little opposition to the introduction of campus speech codes that prohibit speech that 'offends'. In the UK, academics have barely raised a murmur about the introduction of processes and regulations that compromise the free pursuit of knowledge and research. Lecturers now need to ensure that their teaching is consistent with bureaucratically devised 'learning outcomes' that meet the requirements of externally imposed benchmarking criteria. Lecturers are no longer supposed to teach what they think needs to be taught, and they certainly do not have the right

---

[6]   Russell Berman and Stephen Haber, 'Whatever happened to the Academic left?', *Hoover Digest*, 2002, no. 2.

to lecture material for which the learning outcome cannot be demonstrated in advance. Fortunately, despite these formalities, scholars still teach what they think they should teach, but the acceptance of these bureaucratic codes underlines the fragile foundation for academic freedom.

Of course words can offend. But one of the roles of a university is to question conventional truths. The pursuit of ideas has always demanded that intellectuals question the sacred and mention the unmentionable. A civilized intellectual institution teaches its members how *not* to take criticisms personally, and how *not* to be offended by uncomfortable ideas. It also teaches its members how to deal with being offended.

Cavalier attitudes towards free and unfettered debate, and lack of enthusiasm for engagement in controversy, contribute towards the wider sense of political malaise. Instead of countering the public's mood of disengagement, such attitudes provide cultural affirmation for it. The absence of a cultural commitment to debate does not cause the disengagement of the public from the political process, but these two things are inextricably linked. More importantly, the diminishing status of debate underlines the lack of respect that society accords to intellectual clarification.

A disengaged public

Politicians have come to recognize that their political, ideological and moral links with the electorate are fragile. Traditional forms of party politics, political values and identities have little purchase on an evidently disenchanted public. Popular mistrust of authority is confirmed by the growing alienation of people from the system of elections. American-style voting apathy has become a fact of life in the New Europe, where a significant proportion of the electorate believes that voting is a waste of time. The low turnout of voters affects the authority of governments who are keenly sensitive to the erosion of their legitimacy. Unfortunately, the predominant response of politicians is not to seek ways of reconnecting with the public but to avoid the problem through looking for quick-fix solutions.

Increasingly, every election threatens to become an embarrassing reminder of the political wasteland that we inhabit. Apathy is no longer an adequate term of description for the steady erosion of the public's involvement in the political life of the United States. In almost every presidential election since 1960, voter participation has steadily declined – from 62.5 per cent of the electorate in 1960 to 50.1 per cent in 1988. During the election in 1996, only 49 per cent of the voting-age population bothered to cast their ballots – the lowest turn out since 1924. The election in 2000 continued this pattern, with only about 50 per cent of registered voters participating. The alienation of the public from the political process is particularly striking in relation to the election of 2000. Unlike the election of 1996, where the outcome was seen to be a foregone conclusion, the contest in 2000 was the most open for decades. Yet the number of Americans who voted was roughly the same as in 1996. According to the Committee for the Study of the American Electorate, the cumulative effect of voter disengagement during the past 30 years is that today, '25 million Americans who used to vote no longer do so'. Yet voter participation in presidential elections appears positively high compared to the ballots cast for candidates running for a seat in the House of Representatives. These have averaged around 35 per cent in the 1990s.

In the aftermath of 9/11, media pundits speculated that this tragic event and the sense of patriotism to which it gave rise might increase political participation. However, it soon became evident that not even such a major event could disrupt the pre-existing pattern of disengagement. The first 18 primaries prior to 5 July 2002 saw 'not just low turnout, but record low turnout –

with only eight per cent of Democrats and seven per cent of Republicans going to the polls'.[7]

Nor can European commentators feel smug about the political illiteracy of the American electorate. In Britain, the facts speak for themselves. It is worth recalling that back in 1997, New Labour was backed by only 31 per cent of those qualified to vote. Voter turnout at this election was the lowest since 1945. Even the much-hyped public relations campaign surrounding devolution in Scotland and Wales failed to engage the public's interest. Voter participation in these 'history-making' elections in 1999 indicated that the public regarded devolution as another stage-managed event. Only 46 per cent of the Welsh electorate voted, while in Scotland, a high-profile media campaign designed to promote voter participation led to a turnout of 59 per cent, less than two thirds. On the same day, polling booths in England were empty, with only 29 per cent of registered voters turning out for the 6 May local elections. The June 1999 UK elections to the European Parliament brought a turnout of 23 per cent – and in one Sunderland polling station, only 15 people turned up out of the 1000 entitled to vote. In the 2001 General Election, apathy emerged as the dominant issue under debate – and the turnout was an all-time low of 59 per cent. Tony Blair was returned to office with the backing of just 24 per cent of the electorate.

The Brent East by-election in September 2003 is symptomatic of the process of political disengagement. After the Liberal Democrats managed to win this traditional Labour seat, the result was characterized as a 'political earthquake' and the 'biggest hammer blow of Tony Blair's political career'. A closer inspection of this event reveals that this so-called earthquake was produced by a combination of low turnout and voters' cynicism with the government. On a turnout of 36 per cent this was one of the most disengaged high-profile by-elections in British politics.

[7] See Seth Gitell, 'Apathy at the polls', *The Boston Phoenix*, 4 December 2002.

Apathy and disengagement breed both anti-political and apolitical reactions. The political class is aware of this: but instead of attempting to address the underlying malaise and disillusionment through developing challenging political ideals that could inspire the electorate to vote, its response has been to acquiesce in dumbing down. The recall of Governor Gray Davis, and the resulting election of Arnold Schwarzenegger to the governorship of California in 2003, is a testimony to the triumph of political illiteracy in the Anglo-American world. This event was not simply the triumph of personality over politics but the outcome of the inexorable decline of the authority of ideals. Arnie personifies the anti-politician politician, who makes no claims to stand for anything. This recall election may appear as a typically Californian event that could not happen in Europe, but as the French newspaper *Le Figaro* reminded its readers: 'You shouldn't mock Arnold Schwarzenegger; what California invents, America adopts and Europe ends up imitating.'[8]

The steady decline of voter participation is directly linked to a much wider process. Lack of participation provides a clear index of disillusionment and public mistrust in the existing political system. Surveys of American public attitudes indicate that approval of the government has steadily declined in recent decades. Whereas in 1958, over 75 per cent of the American people trusted their government to do the right thing, only 28.2 per cent could express a similar sentiment in 1990. Since the beginning of this decade, trust in politicians has continued to decline. The 1996 survey conducted by Gallup, titled 'In a State of Disunion', found that 64 per cent of the respondents had little or no confidence that government officials tell the truth.

A major study carried out by the Brookings Institution in May 2002 found that not even the wave of patriotism that followed in the aftermath of 9/11 translated into a durable

---

[8]   *Le Figaro*, 7 October 2003.

growth of trust in the US government. This survey showed that whereas in July 2001 only 29 per cent of Americans expressed a positive regard for their government, this figure almost doubled to 57 per cent in the aftermath of 11 September 2001. However, by May 2002, public trust in federal government had fallen back to 40 per cent, and experts felt that the opportunity for the reforging of a relationship of trust had already probably passed.[9]

Surveys in Europe point to a similar pattern. Studies carried out in the European Union indicate that around 45 per cent of the population is dissatisfied with the 'way that democracy works'. In Britain, surveys reveal a high level of public cynicism towards politicians. A Gallup poll conducted in April 1995 concluded that most people's opinion of Members of Parliament was 'low' or 'very low'. A decade previously, only a third of people adopted this view. According to another survey, carried out in 1994, only 24 per cent of the population believed that the British government places the national interest above their party interests.[10] Politicians consistently come at the bottom of the list of professions that the public trusts. A survey published by the ICM in June 1999 found that only 10 per cent of the respondents stated that they trust politicians a lot, 65 per cent a little, and 25 per cent not at all.[11] A study carried out by the BBC in February 2002 indicated that many people under the age of 45 regarded politicians as 'crooks', 'liars' and a 'waste of time'.[12]

During the 1990s, the erosion of public trust was reflected in a national mood of suspicion towards the political system itself. What emerged was a brand of anti-politics, a cynical dismissal of the elected politician and an obsession with sleaze and corruption

---

[9]   Mackenzie and Labiner (2001), pp. 2–3.
[10] J. Curtice and R. Jowell, 'The sceptical electorate', in Jowell, Curtice, Park, Brook and Ahrendt (1995), pp. 141 and 148.
[11] Findings of the poll published in the *Guardian*, 8 June 1999.
[12] 'Politics a "turn-off" for under 45s', *BBC News*, 28 February 2002.

in Westminster and Washington. The Clinton era was one of permanent scandal; and controversy surrounded the manner of Bush's election, only to be followed by a series of corporate scandals culminating in the Enron collapse. New Labour's success at portraying the Conservatives as a party of sleaze was crucial to its electoral success of 1997 – but the New Labour government quickly found that it was not immune to the politics of scandal. A spate of minor scandals involving Labour MPs and ministers followed the 1997 election victory, and the issue of sleaze continued to haunt the government through 1998, as successive ministers were forced to resign. The furore that surrounded Cheriegate in December 2002 – despite the absence of any allegation that the Prime Minister's wife had done anything illegal – indicates that cynicism towards government is a permanent feature of life.

The exhaustion of political life has little to do with political corruption, inept political leaders or insensitive bureaucracies. What has changed during the past two decades is the very meaning of politics itself. At the beginning of the twentieth century, political life was dominated by radically different alternatives. Competing political philosophies offered contrasting visions of the good society. Conflict between these ideologies was often fierce and sometimes provoked violent clashes, even revolutions. 'Left' and 'Right' were no mere labels. In a fundamental sense, they endowed individuals with an identity that said something very important about how they regarded their lives. Ardent advocates of revolutionary change clashed with fervent defenders of the capitalist system, and these competing views dominated the conduct of everyday politics.

The end of the century offered a radically different political landscape. Politics today has little in common with the passions and conflicts that shaped people's commitments and hatreds over the past century. There is no longer room for either the ardent defender of the free-market faith, or the robust advocate of revolutionary transformation. It would be wrong to conclude that politics has become simply more moderate. Politics has gone into early retirement. The big issues of our time – the impending environmental catastrophe, threats to our health, killer bugs, weapons of mass destruction – are presented as perils that stand above politics. It is widely believed that the world is out of control and that there is little that human beings can do to master these developments or influence their destiny. Deprived of choice and options, humanity is forced to acquiesce in a world-view that Margaret Thatcher aptly described as TINA – There Is No Alternative.

If indeed there is no alternative, politics can have little meaning. Without alternatives, debate becomes empty posturing about trivial matters. Politicians are forced to inflate relatively banal proposals to the level of a major policy innovation. This is the age of 'micro-politics', in which politics has adopted the language of technocracy and presents itself through a depoliticized language of managerialism. The growth of a managerial political style has gone hand-in-hand with a shift to the personal. Even protest movements have internalized a highly individualistic and personal style of political vocabulary. 'Not In My Name', the prominent slogan of demonstrators against the 2003 Iraq war, is a statement of personal preference. It does not even purport to engage or convince other people. Not in my name is about me, not you.

Personalities and individual behaviour dominate the presentation of contemporary politics. As public life has become emptied of its content, private and personal preoccupations have been projected into the public sphere. Consequently, passions that were once stirred by ideological differences are far more likely to be engaged by individual misbehaviour, private troubles and personality conflicts. The private lives of politicians excite greater interest than the way they handle their public office. In Britain it is widely noted that the reality TV show *Big Brother* 'arouses passions that politics can no longer stir'.[13] In the US, a television

programme titled *The American Candidate* aims to use the reality
TV format to pick a 'people's candidate' from its contestants. This
format is being adopted in the UK and is likely to be transmitted
before the next general election. With so many people turned off
managerial politics, is it any surprise that politicians are turning
to reality television producers, to learn how to engage with an
uninterested public?

Re-engagement through the lowest common denominator

The disengagement of people from the institutions of society is
the defining feature of contemporary political life. It is also the
principal problem that preoccupies the energies of the political
establishment and the cultural elite. Sadly, these groups have
drawn the conclusion that apathy and cynicism are responses to a
political culture that is too sophisticated and too challenging for
ordinary people. From this standpoint, the political elites have
drawn the conclusion that the way to re-engage is to be less
demanding and less challenging. What is often called the *politics
of inclusion* is a project that is designed to bypass the problem, by
demanding very little of people, and seeking a technical quick-fix
for the political malaise.

Instead of being concerned with the lack of substance of
contemporary politics, the cultural elite believes that the way to
reconnect with the public is through dumbing down further. This
attitude informs the various projects that are designed to contain
the problem of low voter turnout. Instead of attempting to
improve the standard of political discourse or encourage
involvement through debate, politicians and officials seek to

---

[13] See Alice Thomson, 'Politics doesn't have to be like the *Big Brother* House',
Daily Telegraph, 4 December 2002.

make voting as easy and effortless as possible. This project is justified by the dubious assumption that the reason why people don't vote is because they are very busy or because people find the exercise a difficult one. Instead of acknowledging the fact that, for many people, voting is now seen as a pointless effort, there is a tendency to complicate matters by suggesting that electoral participation is a particularly difficult and burdensome task. It appears that travelling to a polling booth, filling in a ballot form and dropping it into a box, is a challenge that severely tests the mental and moral capacity of contemporary adults. So adverts published by Lewisham Council, for the London mayoral election in December 2001, showed a comfortable sofa and a man in a bath, encouraging voters to stay at home and post their ballots. Barry Quirk, chief executive of the Council, advised people to 'simply sit back on the sofa, cast your vote', and added 'it's as easy as that – no more trudging to the polling booth in the rain'.

From the standpoint of democratic ideals, voting involves responsibility and a purposeful intention to make a difference. Today, the ideal that voting implies some kind of a commitment to the democratic process has been subordinated to the pragmatic notion that it should be as effortless an activity as possible. Preferably nothing should be demanded of the voter other than the meaningless act of pushing a button or ticking a box in the comfort of one's home. Predictably, this systematic trivialization of the process of voting is justified on the basis that the electoral process should be as inclusive as possible. Through making a minimal effort, even those who are indifferent to the process can be involved in this caricature of democratic participation. The ideal of the active and interested citizen is increasingly portrayed as a symbol of a bygone elitist era.

At various times, proposals are made to reconnect with the electorate through placing polling booths in supermarkets and other convenient sites, institutionalizing voting via the telephone or the Internet, or text voting, or postal voting. In Britain, electronic voting has been put forward as an instrument for revitalizing the political process. In 2003, e-voting was piloted in English local elections. Predictably, this initiative was proposed on the ground that this was an *inclusive* way forward. Nick Raynsford, the local government minister justified this step in the following terms:

> The electoral pilots aim to improve turnout, in particular among key groups of people who might otherwise be excluded, such as people who are working away from the area, younger voters, the elderly and people with mobility problems.[14]

At a time when very few people believe that there is any point in voting at local elections, the idea that somehow a substantial group of people are 'excluded' by their circumstances is very much the product of the fertile imagination of our cultural elite.

Historical experience demonstrates that when the 'excluded' want to be 'included', they do a very good job of breaking down the barriers to their participation. Restrictions on the right to vote have been swept away by mass movements of workers, women and minority groups. When people believe that voting makes a difference, they rise to the occasion as a politicized public. They do not need electronic solutions that transform the act of voting into a meaningless individualized gesture. As is the case with most initiatives designed to promote inclusion, the object of inclusion is patronized. Just as promoters of inclusion scorn 'elitist' museums, classical education and libraries focused on books, so the advocates of e-voting disparage traditional ways of voting. 'We don't think we can say to people that they can only vote in the traditional way in a rickety booth in a church hall or school using a stubby pencil', declared Raynsford.[15] Through

---

[14] Cited in Simon Parker, 'Cross Culture', *Guardian*, 30 April 2003.
[15] Cited in Simon Parker, 'Cross Culture', *Guardian*, 30 April 2003.

portraying so-called traditional voting as a dreary imposition on the British citizen, Raynsford succeeds in transforming a fundamental feature of democratic life into a burden that no sensible person could tolerate. Voter apathy becomes the fault of cold church halls rather than of the dumbed-down political culture that comes up with such patronizing solutions.

The numerous initiatives dreamt up by the promoters of quick-fix inclusive voting reflect the abandonment of the belief that an active democratic public can be reconstituted. The politics of inclusion is oriented towards the individual rather than a wider section of society. Its various gimmicks – interactivity, postal voting, telephone voting – aim to connect with the people as atomized individuals rather than as an educated public. However, the very individualization of the act of voting deprives it of any meaning. The idea of public duty or communal responsibility is displaced by focusing on individual convenience. Such initiatives can only deactivate, demotivate and further individualize a community. In the May 2000 local elections, the district of Watford in Hertfordshire set up polling booths in shops and permitted the electorate to cast their ballot over the weekend, when fewer would be at work. The outcome? Voter turnout slumped by nearly 10 per cent, to just 27 per cent of the electorate.[16] As an arbitrary, individual act of convenience, the act of voting loses its meaning further still.

Is it any surprise that voting is fast losing its meaning? At a time when the disengagement of the public has become the defining feature of twenty-first-century Western political culture, there are more and more opportunities afforded to people to 'have their say'. Radio and television programmes continually launch new polls. People can vote for their favourite classical record or their favourite pop star. Interactive television and the Internet regularly ask you to have your say about a whole range

---

[16] Cited in Simon Parker, 'Cross Culture', *Guardian*, 30 April 2003.

of issues. The more the act of voting has lost its purpose and meaning, the more desperate attempts are launched to give people yet another opportunity to 'have their say'.

UK commentators have noted, with more than a hint of envy, that more young people vote for their favourite personality on the reality TV programme *Big Brother* than they do in elections. Indeed, it is frequently suggested that politicians have some important lessons to learn from this programme. In a report published by The Hansard Society arguing this point, its author Stephen Coleman, an Oxford academic, observed that politicians need to find exciting ways to use technology to give people more control over how they view the political process. 'The way to liberate political democracy from its current cultural ghetto requires a new conception of two-way accountability; a creative and exciting use of the new technologies of interactivity,' argues Coleman.[17] This techno-fix idea implies that interactivity is in some sense similar to participation and political involvement. From this perspective, children are the easiest to involve – they always want to have their say about their favourite football player or pop star. No wonder numerous British advocacy groups are campaigning to lower the minimum age of voting to 16.

An elitist populism

The tendency to redefine democratic participation using the diffuse notion of 'having your say' is associated with the political agenda of inclusion. This agenda aims to tackle the problem of disengagement through a populist programme that combines flattering people with treating them as children. A project promoting inclusion need have no meaning other than to provide the pretence of participation. That is why the Internet is so often

[17]   Cited in '*Big Brother* Gives Politics Lesson', in *BBC News*, 3 June 2003.

held up as the ideal site for participation by the elitist populism of
our times. The British author George Walden pointed to the
meaningless character of this participation, when he observed: 'of
what advantage is it to democracy that from 1998 the Prime
Minister could pretend to converse directly with individuals,
when in reality all that is happening is that the public's all too
predictable complaints are computed by party officials and a pro-
forma reply, purporting to come from the PM's mouth, is keyed
into the machine?'[18]

In the past, populism was associated with a wider agenda.
Today it seems to have no role other than connecting with
people. Connecting or interacting has become a substitute for
having something to say. Inclusion is its own virtue – it matters
little what one is included in. As I argue in Chapter 5, inclusion
for its own sake also shapes policies such as widening access to
higher education, the arts and culture. Politicians in particular are
drawn towards new infantilizing initiatives designed to 'reconnect' with the public. In Britain, politicians have even consulted
Peter Bazalgette, the creator of the reality TV show *Big Brother*, to
advise them how to connect with younger voters.

Making do with the pretence of participation reflects the low
expectations that the cultural elite has of the public. The Hansard
Society's Stephen Coleman believes that politics 'is too closed and
obscure for most people' and 'they literally do not understand
what is going on'. Behind the populist agenda of inclusion lurks
an elitist contempt for people. Often this contempt is most
pronounced among liberal or left-wing political activists, who
ought to know better. The corollary of the idea that participating
needs to be made less demanding is the notion that people are not
really up to much. Instead of acknowledging the dearth of
political ideas, the public is indicted for being gullible. In the US,
this paternalistic impulse led some Democratic Party activists to

---

[18]   Walden (2001), p. 151.

blame the defeat of their presidential candidate in 2000 on the stupidity of the people. One liberal activist, Michael Gronewalter, states that 'civility and intelligent dialogue are useful tools among intelligent people', but are inappropriate for engaging with the public. He argues:

> I really think the problem is that we as liberals are in general far more intelligent, well-reasoned and educated and will go to astonishingly great lengths to convince people of the integrity and validity of our fair and well thought-out arguments. The audience, in case anyone has been paying attention, *isn't always getting it! I suspect the problem is not the speaker – it is most of the audience.*[19]

According to one of Gronewalter's colleagues, the American public has become a sort of 'Fast Food Electorate', and it is as if 'Americans suffer collectively from a plague of Attention Deficit Disorder'. This negative assessment of the American electorate serves to legitimize his call for dumbing down the Democratic message: 'it is time for liberals to use slogans, sound bytes and photo-ops to marry Bush, his administration and his cronies to their corrupt agenda'.[20]

The view that the public is too stupid to grasp the high-minded and sophisticated ideals of American liberals expresses a profound sense of contempt for human beings. Furthermore, it uncritically transfers responsibility for the contemporary malaise of political life on the uneducated electorate. The direct and transparent denunciation of people's mental capacities, made by the activists cited above, is rare in a culture that is at least outwardly anti-elitist. Usually, such contempt is transmitted through nods, winks and terms like '*Daily Mail* reader', 'white

[19]   Michael Gronewalter, 'Don't Get Smart, Get Stupid', *Democratic Underground.Com*, 13 April 2002.

[20]   Christian Dewar, 'Dumbing Down: America's Fast Food Electorate', *Democratic Underground.Com*, 24 April 2002.

van man', 'Mondco man', 'tabloid readers', 'pebbledash people' and 'Worcester Woman'. In the US the moral superiority of the anti-elitist is affirmed through such terms as 'Nascar dads', 'Valley girls', 'Joe six-pack', 'Redneck', 'dittoheads' or 'salad dodger'. However, what today's cultural elite really thinks of people is most vividly revealed through their attitude towards higher education, culture and other targets of its policy of inclusions. These subjects will be the topics of the following chapters.

4 Social Engineering

Contemporary populism has no wider purpose than to connect with people. Consequently, initiatives designed to increase electoral participation can be entirely indifferent to the intrinsic meaning of the act of voting. Simply pushing a button is sufficient for maintaining the pretence of participation – and if the public lacks the inclination to go to the polling station and vote, for the political elite changing the meaning of voting seems like a small price to pay for maintaining the rate of electoral participation.

The subordination of the democratic act of voting to the objective of retaining contact with people is paralleled throughout cultural life. Nothing seems to have any intrinsic worth. Knowledge, education, higher education, art and culture are not promoted because of any inherent qualities that they may possess. This instrumentalist orientation towards culture is not unprecedented: the commercialization of cultural production has always encouraged an instrumentalist ethos towards intellectual and artistic life. What has changed is that culture is not simply promoted as an economic good, but fervently propagated for advancing the policy of social inclusion. As in the case of voting, culture is valued insofar as it advances the populist agenda of inclusion, participation and access. Increasingly, every aspect of culture is regarded from the standpoint of this agenda. The question is not whether a particular institution or cultural artefact is good or bad, beautiful or ugly, inspiring or uninspiring, but whether it is relevant, accessible or inclusive. Regardless of its content, that which promises to connect with the public can count on the support and affirmation of our cultural elites.

Just as the imperative of social engineering is prepared to change the meaning of voting, so it is ready to endow art, culture, knowledge and the university with a new definition. The imperative to 'connect' leads to a situation where cultural and educational institutions are less likely to be judged according to criteria internal to themselves than on their relevance and accessibility to a wider public. In previous times, so-called High Culture was frequently indicted because it was the monopoly of a small oligarchy and ordinary folk were prevented from enjoying its achievements. Today, the criticism levelled at High Culture is much more likely to take exception to the fact that it is far too demanding to be popular, that it is alien to, and aloof from, people's lives.

Relevance has become a key concept of the contemporary ethos of social engineering. Historically, great thinkers were criticized by populist anti-intellectual demagogues for being out of touch with the needs of the people. The out-of-touch intellectual and artist have been objects of populist derision throughout the past three centuries. Today, this philistine critique has been expanded to embrace any aspect of cultural life that is deemed not directly relevant to the people – which, in practice, means not seen as relevant by policy-makers. Policy-makers and politicians wedded to the imperative of social engineering take great pleasure in attacking major museums and universities for being too stuffy and elitist. Matthew (now Lord) Evans, who was appointed chairman of Resource, the British Government's advisory body on museums, stated in his first major speech in 2000 that museums needed to demonstrate their 'relevance to local communities' by sending their artefacts out to be displayed in shops and pubs.[1] In Britain, smug asides about elitist Oxford

---

[1]   Cited in Nigel Reynolds, 'Art elitist? I never meant to say that', *Daily Telegraph*, 16 October 2003. For a discussion of the new philistine trends in the world of museums, see Appleton (2001).

and Cambridge have become a key component of the staple diet of populist politics. It is as if an object exhibited in a pub becomes a focus of praise because it is in a pub, rather than in the National Gallery.

Once values like relevance and accessibility acquire fundamental importance then they become the arbiters of educational and cultural life. From this perspective, the value of a sociological concept, an opera or a Shakespeare play is determined by its relevance and accessibility. And if it fails to be relevant or accessible it may face a populist makeover in order to make it useful to the project of social engineering. In September 2003, it was reported that the Classical Theater Lab in Los Angeles had begun a series of audience-friendly Shakespeare productions. The series 'Who's Afraid of William Shakespeare?' aims to make productions that are not intimidating for the audience. The actors explain the story as they proceed, paraphrase a lot of the difficult language, and stop to answer questions posed by members of the audience.[2]

The simplification of Shakespeare by the Classical Theater Lab is not motivated by any artistic insights that demand a major reinterpretation of the old master's plays. Reinterpretation of a drama fuelled by changing aesthetic sensibility is part and parcel of the evolution of the theatre. However, in this case reinterpretation is not the outcome of an aesthetic judgement, but of the concern to be relevant to the audience. As in the case of e-voting, it is the desire to develop a relationship with the public, rather than the quality of that relationship, that drives the objective of making Shakespeare more digestible.

Certain forms of cultural practices cannot be simplified and made relevant. It is difficult to turn a complex musical symphony, for instance, into family-friendly entertainment. So instead of a populist makeover, it needs to disappear or to be treated with

[2]   John Weeks, 'At last, art for idiots!', in *U-Daily News*, 29 September 2003.

disdain. A clear example of this is the contemporary critique of the essay. According to some advocates of the access movement, the essay is so elitist that you cannot possibly ask ordinary university students to write one. Richard Winter, Professor of Education at Anglia Polytechnic University, argues that essay writing is 'difficult and alien, especially to those returning to formal learning after a substantial break and those who are first-generation participants in higher education'. Winter believes that the essay 'disenfranchises students who may be quite capable of embodying their understanding of ideas in other genres and styles',[3] and that in any case, the essay is overrated and there other, better, ways for students to learn. Winter prefers what he calls 'patchwork' text assignments: small-scale writing tasks designed to make students feel comfortable and confident.

Winter's rejection of the essay in favour of patchwork text assignments reflects the wider tendency of subordinating education and culture to dictates of social inclusion. Predictably, it is not the impulse of education and the cultivation of the mind that drives this approach but something external to it: the politics of inclusion. The call to displace the essay by patchwork text assignments is motivated by the belief that nothing 'alien' should stand between a student and university learning. This declaration has little to do with the essay form itself. But in the course of promoting patchwork texts, Winter cannot help but disparage the worth of the essay. This example indicates that dumbing down is not an accidental by-product of the campaign to widen access to higher education, but the inevitable consequence of a perspective that views the objective of education as something that is external to education. In this case, access and inclusion is the goal and education is the means to achieve it.

A further example of this trend is the current discussion

---

[3] See Richard Winter, 'Regular writing tasks would aid learning far better than the last-minute essay', *Guardian*, 10 June 2003.

around the public library. The Department for Culture, Media and Sport (DCMS) believes that people may be put off going to the library because it looks too much like ... a library. One DCMS report speculates that librarians might restrict usage by certain people or sections of the community because of their 'inappropriate attitudes and behaviour', 'inappropriate rules and regulations', or 'book stock policies which do not reflect the needs of the community'. *Better Public Libraries*, a report published by the Commission for Architecture and the Built Environment in August 2003, blames 'traditional notions of the book-lending centres' for a 17 per cent fall in library visits. It demands that libraries should become a 'living room of the city':

> New libraries should increasingly be long-stay places for students, a safe haven for children, even a home from home. They should include cafés, lounge areas with sofas, and chill-out zones where young people can watch MTV, read magazines and listen to CDs on listening posts.[4]

In other words libraries can be involved in the provision of just about any service so long as it is not the tedious business of lending people books. Since getting as many people as possible to walk through the doors of the library is the principal objective, anything that stands in the way of interesting the punters becomes the problem. Books from libraries, like essays from universities, will just have to disappear.

The premise behind *Better Public Libraries* and the policy of access is that any barriers put up by cultural life to people's involvement is a problem to be removed. More broadly, just about any educational or cultural practice that the public does not spontaneously embrace may be stigmatized as elitist. From this perspective, culture is at its best when it can be spoon-fed and

---

[4]   Cited in Martin Wainwright, 'Libraries Blamed for Their Own Decline', *Guardian*, 18 August 2003.

consumed by anyone at any time. But a university discipline, like
a cultural practice, has an integrity of its own. And because this
endows a book or a painting with its own identity, it necessarily
puts up a barrier to spontaneous access. As the British cultural
critic Josie Appleton argues, 'anything that has its own identity
puts up "barriers" – the fact that it resists you makes you aware
that it is a separate object and not your own reflection'. Appleton
adds that 'a painting resists the viewer because it has its own
logic' and warns 'you can't "get it" immediately when you look
at it, you can't take it in one gulp'.[5]

Appleton's argument also extends to institutions. 'Any
institution with any atmosphere at all, such as a library or a
museum, is going to put up a kind of "barrier" and will prevent
you from feeling as if you are in your living room', she observes.
Why? Because a cultural institution has its own sense of itself, its
own collection, its own story and integrity. The barriers they
represent are integral to cultural life, and this is in fact what
makes them attractive to people. Institutions such as a university
also create barriers that need to be overcome by those committed
to their intellectual development. Of course those barriers can be
removed, but at the cost of losing the integrity of higher
education.

Participation in the arts and education is valued because it is
believed that it serves to help people engage with the institutions
of society. According to one advocate of the social inclusion
agenda:

New confidence and skills; new friendships and social
opportunities; cooperation towards achievement; involvement
in consultation and local democracy; affirmation and questioning of identity; strengthening commitment to place;
intercultural links, positive risk-taking – these ... are crucial

---

[5]   Private manuscript to be published as *The Missing Plinth*.

means of fighting social exclusion. Participation in the arts does this partly by building individual and community competence, but more importantly by building belief in the possibility of positive social change.[6]

Governments throughout history have attempted to mobilize the arts to further political ends. Previously, they were used to celebrate national glory; today they are used to establish a point of contact with atomized, and often marginalized, individuals, and this strategy is deployed in a systematic and highly individualized way.

It is important to realize that the populist imperative of social engineering is neither a democratic nor an egalitarian response to the problem of social inequality or poverty. As I noted in the previous chapter, this is a project that aims to re-engage an increasingly fragmented society. Social inclusion, accessibility and participation are part of an agenda that aims to establish points of contact between the cultural elite and an otherwise estranged public. Since establishing contact constitutes the dominant objective, the question of what exactly the excluded are included *in* is seldom explored. It is easier to widen participation than to ensure that what people participate in is worthy of their involvement.

Paradoxically, policies of social engineering are generally presented as part of a programme of radical reform. This is certainly how widening participation in higher education is promoted. Yet the idea that the university is experiencing a programme of reform is a very strange one. Reforms in other spheres of life do not proceed on the assumption that the institution they are about to create will become inferior to the one that preceded it. In the postwar period, universal access to health care through the establishment of the National Health Service

---

[6]   F. Matarosso,'Use or Ornament? The Social Impact of Participation in the Art', *Comedia*, 1997.

(NHS) did not mean that the hospital was turned into a first-aid station, in the way that the university has been reinvented as a college of further education.

There is nothing new about attempting to subject culture and education to the agenda of social engineering. Critics in previous eras took issue with the celebration of art for its own sake, and disparaged the idea of the disinterested pursuit of the truth. The difference now is the way in which such attitudes are systematically conveyed and applied in all parts of social life, and the degree of reluctance to uphold any institutional values and standards at all. Accordingly today, by their very nature, institutional values and standards are obstacles to widening access, and an elitist insult to the self-esteem of the excluded.

In principle, creating equal opportunities for all is a worthwhile objective. Increasing public participation in intellectual and cultural life is a goal that anyone with democratic leanings can strongly support. It is not the case that, as conservative cultural critics have often argued, popular participation must be to the detriment of standards. The belief that 'more means worse' was, for example, the basis of Kingsley Amis' objection to the expansion of the numbers of university students in the 1960s.[7] Rather, the expansion of higher education will only lead to a fall in standards if widening participation is driven by concerns that have little to do with the promotion of the ideals of the university. It is when education and culture are dominated by concerns that are external to their agenda that more does indeed mean less.

Despite its populist rhetoric, the social exclusion agenda is deeply hostile to genuine popular culture. Genuine popular culture is self-generated rather than the product of policies that aim to engage the public. Social exclusion policies, by contrast, aim to shape public taste, standardize it and ultimately control it.

---

[7]   Amis is cited in Shils (1972).

The attack on autonomy

As with education, cultural and arts policy has been mobilized to combat social exclusion. This instrumental deployment of cultural policy is in striking contrast to the idea that culture possesses a measure of autonomy, indeed that it should be a self-contained realm that develops in accordance with its own laws. Social engineering now shapes public policy on culture. The Department for Culture, Media and Sport seeks to make cultural resources accessible to 'the many, not just the few', and to rebrand cultural institutions as 'centres for social change'.[8] Using cultural institutions to connect the political establishment to people turns these bodies towards an objective that has little to do with their original reason for existence, and as such represents a direct challenge to their institutional independence.

Promoters of social engineering argue that institutional autonomy is no big deal since it rarely exists in practice. They sometimes contend that the quest for autonomy represents the policy of vested interests, and suggest that the idea of institutional independence, like that of knowledge for its own sake, is a sham that overlooks the fact that cultural institutions are subservient to the interests of the ruling elites. They claim that the university's traditional demand for institutional autonomy represents a claim to preserve the privileges of the already privileged. Thus, undermining the autonomy of the university is a step in the right direction, since it facilitates the project of widening access. Without diminishing its institutional independence, it is not possible to subject the university to the externally imposed demands of the social engineering agenda. That is why the access movement is so enthusiastic about getting rid of features of university life that distinguish it from other sectors of education. According to one advocate of this approach, getting rid of the

---

[8]   See DCMS (2000).

boundary that separates higher from other forms of education is necessary for encouraging greater access. Hence 'the strength, stability and clarity' of the boundaries between higher education and others 'have been questioned at different points and to various degrees by alternative access routes and relationships which anticipate new audiences and broader purposes for a "higher" education'.[9]

Breaking down 'the strength, stability and clarity' of the boundary that separates the university from the rest of society represents a self-conscious attempt to undermine the university's aspiration to institutional autonomy. In Britain, this crusade is justified on the grounds that the university serves the narrow self-interest of a powerful elite; in the US, on the grounds that the university has never been, and never will be, devoted to the pursuit of disinterested knowledge. A powerful mood of cultural cynicism drives critics to denounce the claim for autonomy. As Russell Berman, Professor in Humanities at Stanford University, wrote, today's cultural cynics 'cannot imagine a knowledge *not* complicitous with power, a science *not* dependent on the Pentagon, or teachers *not* driven solely by self-interest'.[10] Of course the critics have a point. Universities like other cultural institutions have done many things other than the disinterested pursuit of knowledge. They have on occasions served dubious economic and political agendas. However, as Berman argues, 'a critique of the universities that omits the possibility of a life of the mind is, ultimately, just anti-intellectualism'.[11]

A critique of the university that precludes the possibility of genuine search for knowledge represents an acquiescence to a

[9] Gareth Parry, 'Marking and Mediating the Higher-Education Boundary', in Fulton (1989), p. 24.

[10] Russell A. Berman, 'Perestroika for the University!', *Telos*, 81 (Fall 1989), p. 115.

[11] Russell A. Berman, 'Perestroika for the University!', *Telos*, 81 (Fall 1989), p. 115.

perpetual climate of intellectual malaise. Yet the feeble founda-
tions for institutional independence do not constitute an
argument against trying to achieve a measure of autonomy. They
merely point to the difficulty of approximating the *ideal* of
intellectual and cultural autonomy: and the defence of such an
ideal is central to the development of a healthy society. One of the
most persuasive arguments in favour of autonomy has been
mounted by the recently deceased leftist French sociologist Pierre
Bourdieu. Bourdieu recognizes that the claim for institutional
autonomy represents a demand for a privileged status. But he
argues that 'cultural producers', as he calls them, 'can do this
without remorse or moral hesitation since, by defending
themselves as a whole they defend the universal'. Bourdieu
argues for the defence of the 'economic and social conditions
necessary for the autonomy of different fields of cultural
production', because such autonomy provides the platform from
which ideas expressing the general interests of society can be
produced.[12]

Bourdieu's strong defence of autonomy is not motivated by the
objective of distancing the university from society by turning it
into an ivory tower. Autonomy is valued because it creates a
space where cultural producers can function without being
subordinated to any external interests. However, this work is
directed towards society, and autonomy is prized because it
provides a stable foundation for the kind of cultural and
intellectual life that is worthy of society's needs.

A weaker defence of autonomy is offered by the Scottish
philosopher Gordon Graham. Graham too values academic
autonomy. But he is concerned that if it becomes an end in
itself, and if the ideas generated through it fail to have an impact
on society, then its value becomes questionable. 'Academic

---

[12] Pierre Bourdieu, 'The Corporatism of the Universal: The Role of
Intellectuals in the Modern World', *Telos* 81 (Fall 1989), p. 103.

autonomy, which crucially includes freedom of thought and inquiry, is rendered much less valuable than it might be if the thinking it protects has little or no influence on the general formation of social ideas', he writes.[13] Graham is of course right that society will not protect that which it does not value. As both Bourdieu and Graham recognize, in the end intellectuals and artists have to create ideas and objects of value for a wider society. But they do not create it on demand or in response to external pressure, but through the inner dynamic and the external interaction of specific cultural fields.

Despite the prevailing mood of philistinism, proponents of the social engineering agenda are from time to time still forced to pay lip-service to the ideal of valuing culture for its own sake. 'We should not lose sight of the fact that participation in sporting and cultural activities are an end in themselves and enrich people's lives every single day', states the DCMS 2003 Annual Plan. However, such statements are swiftly subordinated to a more instrumentalist approach towards the arts. It appears that the arts are important for 'improving [educational] attainment and behaviour, and encouraging lifelong learning; helping to combat crime and create safe, active and cohesive communities, [and] ... making a very substantial contribution to the economy'.[14] Such instrumentalist appreciation of the arts introduces criteria for assessing it that has nothing to do with its own qualities. Through focusing on the impact of art on a variety of social issues, it ceases to be judged according to standards internal to art, and thereby loses its ability to determine its own direction.

Bourdieu believed that one of the main sites of struggle for intellectuals is over the question of how the worth of their work is

[13] Graham (2002), p. 122.
[14] Cited by Adrian Ellis, 'Valuing Culture; A Background Note', paper for 'Agenda for Valuing Culture', conference organized by DEMOS, London, 17 June 2003.

assessed. He warned that the 'most serious danger, however, is the tendency to strip intellectuals of their prerogatives to evaluate themselves and their production according to their own criteria'.[15] Once the value of cultural and intellectual work is determined by institutions external to the domain of cultural production, it becomes subject to influences that encourage conformism and bureaucratization. One symptom of this regrettable turn of events is that culture and education are increasingly quantified and measured, rather than valued.

Traditionally, artists and intellectuals have been sensitive to the demands placed on their activities through commercial pressures. In response, they have attempted to insulate their activities from these pressures in order to retain a measure of control over their work. Unfortunately, this self-conscious reaction is relatively feeble in response to political pressures, and there has been little opposition mounted by today's intellectuals and artists to prevent the introduction of bureaucratic or market-driven evaluation of their work. As a result, evaluation in accordance with criteria that is external to intellectual and cultural endeavour has proceeded with alarming speed. Directors of museums and art galleries have tended to roll over and accept the attempts of policy-makers to evaluate cultural institutions in accordance with an agenda that has nothing to do with intellectual or artistic development. One example of this instrumental approach towards culture is a recently announced scheme involving the arts and a community organization in Cleveland, Ohio, which aims to discover whether the arts can help children avoid drugs and risky behaviour. The local arts group has been assigned the task of creating an arts curriculum for 300 African-American youth ages 11–14 to see whether involvement in the arts 'helps participants increase their

---

[15] Pierre Bourdieu, 'The Corporatism of the Universal: The Role of Intellectuals in the Modern World', *Telos* 81 (Fall 1989), p. 106.

self-esteem, self-expression and other attributes that help prevent HIV and AIDS infection'.[16]

In the US, the arts are also promoted on the grounds that they help heal conflict and bring the community together. 'It's becoming more evident than ever that culture not only nourishes but heals, and that it is a significant stabilizing force for a society under duress', observed one art critic in the aftermath of 9/11. He added: 'as maintaining the viability of American steel mills is necessary for defence, keeping our cultural base vital is essential for the country's spirit'. The idea that art serves a therapeutic role is frequently communicated by members of the cultural establishment. After 9/11, Philippe de Montebello, director of New York's Metropolitan Museum, compared his institution with that of a hospital. Hospitals are there to 'fix the body', he remarked: 'we're here to fix the soul'.[17]

There has been little objection from artists and cultural workers to British Government ministers' claims that the arts are 'good for your health'; that 'the arts have a key role in making our society a better place to live'; or that the arts 'can help tackle crime'.[18] The Arts Council and local cultural services have swiftly internalized the agenda of social inclusion. Thus the director of Leisure and Cultural Services at Wigan Council promotes the benefits of sports, art and play on the grounds that these activities 'improve cognitive and social skills; reduce impulsiveness and risk-taking behaviours; raise self-esteem and self-confidence and improve education and employment prospects'.[19] The government has established a special team of advisors called a PAT

---

[16] *The Plain Dealer*, 23 October 2003.
[17] Cited in Mary Thomas, 'For a shared expression of emotions, we turn to the arts', *Pittsburgh Post-Gazette*, 11 November 2001.
[18] Cited in Sara Selwood 'Measuring Culture', *Spiked-online*, 30 December 2002.
[19] See 'Realising the potential for cultural services', Wigan Council, 17 December 2001.

(Policy Action Team), which specializes in policies that target social exclusion through raising the self-esteem of the excluded. The Policy Action Team 10 social inclusion report to the DCMS acknowledged the potential problems with subordinating cultural services to demands of therapeutic recognition. 'We do not believe that every artist or sportsperson should be a social worker by another name, or that artistic or sporting excellence should take second place to community regeneration', it noted.[20] However, artistic excellence was conspicuously absent from the examples of best practice that the report promoted. One scheme praised by PAT 10 was a centre in Manchester, where people recovering from mental illness 'find that the arts are not merely a powerful antidote to loneliness, but also a significant means of self-fulfilment and of giving pleasure to others'.[21] This goal of transforming Britain's cultural institutions into centres for therapeutic engagement with excluded people is one of the clearest illustrations of the project to reorient them towards the demands of social policy. The lack of public opposition to this policy also indicates that many people working in this sector have little problem with becoming absorbed into the new cultural bureaucracy.

To ensure that these objectives are achieved, the DCMS is keenly interested in evaluating the impact that its policies are having. As the cultural theorist Sara Selwood, argues: 'the gathering of evidence about the impact of the arts has assumed centre-stage in cultural policy'.[22] In a similar vein, the university has become one of the most intensely audited institutions in society. Every aspect of university life, from teaching, to student progression, to modes of assessment and research, are now systematically audited. One of the direct consequences of this

---

[20] *Building on PAT 10 – Progress Report on Social Inclusion,* February 2001,
      p. 5.
[21] ibid., p. 22.
[22] Sara Selwood, 'Measuring Culture', *Spiked-online*, 30 December 2002.

process is the erosion of the autonomy of the university. Academics are now expected to work according to criteria established by the external auditor, civil servant and politicians. Auditing does not merely measure: it alters and ultimately transforms how a university works. This development is described by Shore and Wright in the following terms:

Audit heralded a significant break with the principle of academic autonomy. Rather than attacking university autonomy head on, the government concealed the extent of its intervention by recruiting a host of intermediary agencies and by mobilizing academics themselves as managerial professionals and active accomplices in this process.[23]

Auditing leads to the colonization of higher education by the educational bureaucracy. Colonization works best through collaborators and the system of auditing is directed to the task of creating a coterie of experts who police the auditing process. As Shore and Wright note: 'central to the development of new political technologies in higher education has been the creation of new categories of experts including "educational development consultants", "quality assurance officers", "staff development trainers" and "teaching quality assessors"'.[24]

The new group of auditors inside cultural and educational institutions play an active role in weakening the integrity of the intellectual activity pursued. As Pierre Bourdieu noted, their loyalty is not to the institution but to the external system of auditing: 'Thanks to their activities, extraneous norms replace those particular to a given field of cultural production'.[25] The

---

[23] See Chris Shore and Susan Wright, 'Coercive accountability; the rise of audit culture in higher education', in Strahern (2000), p. 68.

[24] See Chris Shore and Susan Wright, 'Coercive accountability; the rise of audit culture in higher education', in Strahern (2000), p. 62.

[25] Pierre Bourdieu, 'The Corporatism of the Universal: The Role of Intellectuals in the Modern World', *Telos* 81 (Fall 1989), p. 105.

auditing ethos forces individuals to submit to a regime that seeks to quantify and inspect their efforts, promoting bite-sized, easily standardized effort that can be easily measured, weighed and served to an infantilized public.

Social engineering and the market

What is the worst insult that can be directed at a university? Probably that it is an elitist ivory tower, out of touch with the real world. Yet there was a time when the opposite accusation was more hurtful. Thirty years ago, the radical historian E. P. Thompson could think of no better way of condemning his institution than to label it Warwick University Ltd. The things that Thompson disliked about Warwick – its corporate structure, its cosy relationship to business, and its obsession with training students for the job market – are today seen as entirely desirable. The modern university does not remain proudly aloof from the business world, but gets stuck into licensing new inventions, consulting with corporations and spinning out high-tech companies.

Traditionally the power of the market has been seen as the main threat to academic autonomy and artistic integrity. The tension between the world of the intellectual and that of business has been widely commented on. For example, the dissidence of intellectuals is explained by the French political theorist Bertrand de Jouvenal as a consequence of an inevitable conflict between the values of the business classes and creative artists. Business is institutionally committed to giving its clientele what they want. By contrast, the creative artist views the worth of his products independently of their market value. As de Jouvenal states: 'the businessman offers to the public "goods" defined as anything the public will buy; the intellectual seeks to teach what is "good", and to him some of the goods offered are things of no value which the public should be discouraged from wanting'.[26]

Historical studies of the university recognize that there has often been a conflict between the values of business and trade, and the pursuit of academic work. From the standpoint of business, the customer is always right. It is not the job of a trader to question or criticize the tastes and values of potential customers. Academics, however, are frequently educating their students' tastes and encouraging them to question their values. Indeed one of the most distinct and important features of academic and intellectual activity is precisely that which cannot be dominated by an instrumental ethos. Academic pedagogy – unlike the service provided by a language school – does not seek to offer what the customer wants, but attempts to provide what the student needs. Artists who produce great art do not ask the question 'what does the public want?' They seek to express something through their art, rather than merely produce an object for sale.

The tension between the values of the business classes and creative artists has made many intellectuals weary of the influence of the market. Commercial and business pressure has always been seen as a potential threat to the exercise of academic and artistic integrity. The market is indifferent to the intrinsic merit of a cultural product – it is interested only in its monetary worth. Commercial considerations create strong pressures towards the popularization of art forms and ideas. That is why advocates of social inclusion often attempt to harness market forces to drive forward their own project – through emptying educational and cultural institutions of any intrinsic worth, market forces can direct them towards objectives set externally by the social engineering agenda.

The capacity of the market to erode the autonomy and

---

[26] Cited in De G. B. Huszar (1960), p. 395.

integrity of the university was noted by Peter Scott, the former editor of *The Times Higher Education Supplement,* when he contrasted previous attitudes towards the university with those that prevailed in the 1990s:

> Then higher education was seen as something to be deserved, to be aspired to; now it is increasingly regarded as something to be purchased by the prudent or fortunate. There is now a powerful movement away from the idea of higher education as a public service. It is no longer to be seen as a cultural, even moral, enterprise in which the notion of intellectual authority plays a key role, but as an economic enterprise in which customers, whether students or others, are enabled to buy services.[27]

This shift of focus may indeed help to reduce the obstacles to wider access. For if higher education is stripped of its deeper cultural significance and is regarded in more commonplace instrumental terms, there is less need to regulate access to the system. This point is clearly understood by sections of the access movement who regard market forces as a useful counterweight against institutional autonomy. The mass market is seen as an ally that would force the university to yield to the demands of populist social engineering.[28]

The convergence between the ethos of consumerism and the agenda of inclusion has helped forge a formidable power that continually impacts on institutions of culture and education. This synthesis of consumerism and populism provides legitimation for the social engineering agenda. Consumer choice and individual access merge into a populist ethos that regards culture and education as consisting of bite-size commodities that can be spoon-fed to Joe Public.

---

[27] Peter Scott, 'Post-binary access and learning', in Parry and Wake (1990), pp. 30–1.

[28] This argument is advanced in Peter Wright, 'Putting learning at the Centre of Higher Education', in Fulton (1989).

Although advocates of the marketization of culture tend to be suspicious of government-led policies of social engineering, they too regard the erosion of cultural and academic autonomy as, on balance, a positive development. From their standpoint, the assimilation of cultural institutions into the market has led to an artistic and intellectual renaissance. Like the proponents of the inclusion agenda, the advocates of the marketization of culture reject the idea that we are going through a period of philistinism. Rather than dumbing down, they claim that society is wising up. This thesis is argued with force by Tyler Cowen, who in his book *In Praise of Commercial Culture* claims that the free market does the best job of promoting cultural excellence. As a result of the workings of the capitalist market, he argues, the United States is going through a cultural renaissance able to provide a 'parade of successful and diverse cultural products'.[29]

Market advocates such as Cowen sustain their thesis by pointing to the quantitative expansion of cultural life in the US. One of his supporters argues that 'during the past *few decades, we have been experiencing what can aptly be* called a "cultural boom": a massive increase in art, music, literature, video, and other forms of creative expression'.[30] This increase in the consumption of cultural goods, which is linked to the growth of prosperity, is seen as evidence of the contemporary boom of culture. There is little doubt that the consumption of culture had become a dynamic feature of contemporary society – however, evidence of increasing cultural consumption tells us little about the quality of what is being consumed. This focus on consumption confuses the public's aspiration for entertainment and distraction with the development of ideas and art. As Hannah Arendt noted back in the sixties, what we have is not mass culture

---

[29] Cowen (2000).
[30] Nick Gillespie, 'All Culture, All the Time', in *Reason*, April 1999.

'but mass entertainment, feeding on the cultural objects of the world'.[31]

Arendt took the view that the marketization of cultural products leads to their degradation, warning that 'culture is being destroyed in order to yield entertainment'. She added:

> The result of this is not disintegration but decay, and those who promote it are not the Tin Pan Alley composers but a special kind of intellectual, often well read and well informed, whose sole function is to organize, disseminate, and change cultural objects in order to persuade the masses that *Hamlet* can be as entertaining as *My Fair Lady*, and perhaps as educational as well. There are many great authors of the past who have survived centuries of oblivion and neglect, but it is still an open question whether they will be able to survive an entertaining version of what they have to say.[32]

Arendt's warnings about the 'special kind of intellectual' who peddles *Hamlet* as a product of entertainment have proved to be prescient. The instrumental orientation towards art and education dominates contemporary cultural life. The main problem today, however, is not the expansion of the entertainment industry, but the crusade to spoon-feed culture to the public led by the social inclusion agenda.

Although Arendt's misgivings about the capture of culture by the entertainment industry need to be taken seriously, her pessimism cannot account for the flourishing of intellectual and artistic life alongside and in interaction with mass entertainment. Cultural life exists in a relation of uneasy tension with the market and, despite the pressure of commerce, intellectuals and artists have been able to create and develop ideas. There is little doubt that today, as in the past, the commercial imperative works

---

[31] Arendt (1993); originally written as 'The Crisis in Culture' in 1961.
[32] Arendt (1993), 'The Crisis in Culture'.

towards commodifying knowledge and art. Nevertheless, the market also provides opportunities for creativity and can provide space, albeit limited, for the pursuit of excellence. The problem today is not the growth of stupefying entertainment but the lack of affirmation for the promotion of intellectual and artistic standards. Commerce does not have a view on what kind of exhibit a museum should show, or whether university students should or should not write essays. The social inclusion agenda, however, is prepared to use both political influence and market forces to achieve its objective. The imperative of social engineering, rather than the market, today represents the greatest threat to the integrity of intellectual and cultural production. Compared to the politics of inclusion, the problems posed by the entertainment industry pale into insignificance.

5   The Culture of Flattery

There is now a barely contested consensus within the cultural and education establishment that access and social inclusion should be at the heart of the missions of cultural institutions. At conferences, officials and administrators routinely demand that universities, libraries, museums and galleries should place inclusion at the centre of their activities. Those seeking a career in the educational or cultural industry frequently boast that they have succeeded in transforming their institution into one that has eliminated all barriers to participation. The barriers they have in mind are not only physical obstacles to disabled access, or monetary costs that may deter the poor from paying for the price of entry, but the intellectual challenge facing people participating in educational and cultural activities. 'Once they were called museums,' notes a review of interactivity in museums in San Francisco. 'Now they're more like amusement parks.'[1]

In Britain, there is a systematic attempt to reorient the cultural institutes from dealing with serious subjects to mounting exhibitions that are directly accessible to people. 'For a variety of reasons people think galleries are too imposing, or that art has little or no relevance to their lives, is elitist, or simply boring', observes a report by the Tyne and Wear Museum. The solution proposed by this Museum is to provide the public with what the cultural elite believes people can handle. It has adopted access

---

[1]   See Steven Winn, 'Interactive Museums', *San Francisco Chronicle*, 19 July 2003.

policies that have 'encouraged the display of works from the collections which may not necessarily be famous or highly regarded, but have been chosen by members of the public simply because they like them or because they arouse certain emotions or memories'.[2] This approach is vigorously pursued by the DCMS, and all the projects it funds now have to publish access targets and detail measures by which they are 'widening access to a broad cross-section of the public for example by age, social class, and ethnicity'.[3] Not surprisingly institutions are attempting to meet access targets by any means that work. Cafés, meeting places, computer facilities and interactive entertainment are considered legitimate activities to get more people to walk through the doors. 'An ace caff with quite a nice museum attached' was the slogan of Saatchi and Saatchi's ad campaign for the V&A. This sums up the attitude of the cultural establishment towards its own institutions. It is now never clear whether museums are masquerading as drop-in centres, or community centres pretending to be museums

Whereas the cultural establishment is intensely proud of its accomplishment of turning museums into community memorials or interactive amusement parks, those who run higher education are still slightly abashed about advertising the fact that they are in the business of transforming universities into high schools. University students are increasingly treated as customers leading to what the American sociologist George Ritzer has called the McDonaldization of the university. As consumers, students are implicitly encouraged to adopt the passive attitude of receiving a service, rather than actively participating in their studies. As a result the conceptual difference between studying in a university and being taught in a school has become blurred. As Gordon

[2]   See www.culture.gov.uk/pdf/musums.pdf + %22museums + for + the + many %22&hl = en&ieUTF-8.
[3]   *Museums for the Many*, DCMS, 1999

Graham notes there is a qualitative difference between these activities: 'while *pupils* are for the most part directed by others, *students* are expected to be much more self-directed'.[4] Sadly, in many institutions, university teaching rarely promotes the kind of self-directed studying that involves the journey of discovery.

In the United States, the McDonaldization of the university has evolved in a haphazard manner in response to market pressure. In the UK this development has been more systematically implemented through a centralized higher education system. Auditing agencies like the Institute for Learning and Teaching in Higher Education have fostered a climate in which teaching has become standardized, and reduced to the role of providing students with easily digestible spoonfuls of information. This process is most clearly symbolized by the ascendancy of the 'handout culture'. Lecture notes transmitted through the web, and numerous other teaching aids, form the staple diet of many university students' learning experience. This so-called inclusive pedagogy is sometimes rationalized on the ground that it helps students overcome unnecessary barriers such as reading serious scholarly monographs. Such dumbed-down practices are presented as part of a new student-centred curriculum.

Flattering students is fast becoming an important institutional norm. Students are frequently not expected to study but to learn. Because complex ideas are not in fact learned, but studied, the intellectual horizon of the learner is restricted to the assimilation of information and the acquisition of skills. In principle, every teaching technique is worth a try. But the manner in which the ILT promotes its student-centred techniques indicates that its main objective is to keep students engaged and happy. For example, group work is used in a way similar to 'circle-time' in primary education. While this technique may make sense when used with five-year-olds, in the university it serves to distract

---

[4]   Graham (2002), p. 36.

students from gaining knowledge through intellectual struggle and hard work. In effect the inclusive agenda infantilizes university students. The role of academics, meanwhile, is to 'support' rather than transform undergraduates. Academics are discouraged from acting as teachers: they, too, are labelled learners on new 'student-centred' campuses.

Widening access to education is not a novel idea. Social reformers in the Victorian era, for example John Ruskin, argued that the working classes should be included in education so that all could appreciate the wonders of human intellectual endeavour. What is distinct about the access movement today is that it is entirely focused on the opening up of educational opportunities while being quite indifferent to the intellectual content of the experience. The access movement makes no pretence of aspiring to an intellectual ideal. Its pedagogy self-consciously eschews cultivating people's appreciation of humanity's cultural achievements, by emphasizing inclusion rather than education, and striving to appeal to the lowest common denominator of the public's imagination. The access movement is profoundly hostile to pedagogic practices, standards and expectations that distinguish the university from other types of educational institutions. Research presented to the European Access Network in July 2001 criticized the 'enormous differences between the approaches and cultures of community education, further education and higher education'.[5] The project of re-launching the university as a community college of further education represents the height of ambition of the access movement.

The aspiration of inclusion is not a new focus for policy-making. Previous political regimes sought to use the institutions of culture and education to integrate different sections of society into a symbolic community. However, such policies were justified

[5]   Cited in Claire Fox, 'The Massification of Higher Education', in Hayes and Wynyard (2002), p. 139.

on the grounds that they helped raise the level of public culture. For example, the nineteenth century British elite sought to give institutional expression to high aesthetic standards in order to assist the task of social integration. 'The highest instruments of human cultivation are also ultimate guarantees of public order', stated Gladstone.[6] Gladstone and his associates took the view that refining public taste would lead to moral improvement, which in turn would assist the integration of the unpredictable masses into the social order. However manipulative and instrumental their motivation, at least the public gained access to some decent museums and art galleries as a result. Today, the policy of inclusion makes no attempt to cultivate and elevate the public taste. On the contrary, it regards the taste of the public as something to flatter and institutionalize. In place of social integration it makes do with providing interactive entertainment for an otherwise disengaged public. 'In the past, people tended to view museums as equivalent to schools', decries Maeryta Medrano, co-founder of Gyroscope Inc., an Oakland-based company that designs interactive exhibits for museums around the US. Medrano is in the business of making sure that museums become Disneyfied, and seems delighted that more and more museums 'have become places where people have a kind of shared social experience'.[7] 'A kind of shared social experience' turns out to be a roundabout way of saying that customers of the Disneyfied museum share the experience of interacting with the gadgets favoured by today's cultural entrepreneurs.

The cultural politics of the nineteenth century are today often castigated as paternalistic and elitist. In this vein, British historian Stefan Collini states that 'this model had its paternalist side – the mandarins knew what was worth having more of whether people

6   Cited in Minihan (2001), p. 36.
7   Cited in Steven Winn, 'Interactive Museums', *San Francisco Chronicle*, 19 July 2003.

clamoured for it or not'.[8] There is little doubt it was not popular demand, but the belief that certain forms of culture could uplift public taste, which motivated Gladstone and his colleagues. Theirs was very much a top-down policy of cultivating public attitudes consistent with the prevailing cultural norms of the Victorian elite. However, it is necessary to note that today's social inclusion policy is no more democratic than its nineteenth-century counterpart. Social inclusion is not a response to popular demand. There are no masses of people demonstrating to be included in the museums, universities and art galleries that have adopted the agenda of social inclusion. The very language in which inclusion policies are framed – 'learning outcomes', 'lifelong learning', 'reinforcing self-esteem' – is one that most people would find incomprehensible. These are words invented by cultural mandarins for use in their bureaucratic world. Many of the recently created cultural institutions that have been launched as self-consciously populist initiatives have failed to attract public support. The Millennium Dome indicates that it takes more than the institutionalization of inclusiveness to attract people's interest. The technologically sophisticated, but dumbed-down, exhibitions at Bradford Cathedral have proved to be a flop, as has an expensively built museum devoted to the celebration of popular music in Sheffield.

'Why do we continue to build certain cultural institutions such as museums at an accelerating rate?' is the question posed by two proponents of the cultural inclusion agenda.[9] There is a variety of motifs for the growth of the museum industry – urban regeneration, the promotion of tourism, the imperative of creating new symbols of community and the dictates of social engineering. But whatever drives the growth of this sector, it is certainly not popular demand. Indeed many of these projects

---

[8]   See Stefan Collini, 'HiEdBiz', *London Review of Books*, 6 November 2003.
[9]   See Pachter and Landry (2001), p. 37.

justify their existence on the grounds that they can create a demand for inclusion. Often policies of inclusion are oriented towards creating incentives for people who are indifferent to what's on offer to sign up to the inclusion agenda. This process of attempting to create a demand for inclusion is particularly striking in higher education. There, officials openly write about creating an aspiration to participate in higher education among those who lack such an ambition. In June 2001, a statement on widening participation issued by Universities UK observed that 'the key issue for the sector now is attracting people with no background of (or current aspirations to) study in HE to courses and universities'. In other words, widening participation has little to do with meeting a real demand for a place in a university. It means getting people to come to university regardless of whether or not they have such aspirations.

Inclusion is a policy peddled by bureaucrats for reasons that have little to do with culture or education. Its approach is no less top-down than that of its nineteenth-century predecessors. The policy is driven by officials who think they know best what the public needs, while pretending to be responding to public opinion. But what distinguishes this approach is its total disregard for both public demand and for concerns that are genuinely cultural or educational in character. At least Gladstone and his colleagues sometimes sought to cultivate and inspire the public imagination. The one-dimensional approach of the inclusion agenda is simply to flatter it.

Inclusion through affirmation

Social inclusion is one of those fashionable concepts like transparency and accountability, which everyone uses but rarely defines. Virtually every policy claims to be inclusive, and it is rare to hear any figure of authority attack attempts to institutionalize social inclusion. As a result, social inclusion is generally accorded the status of a public virtue. As noted previously, policies of inclusion are underwritten by the political elite's desire to establish or re-establish a point of contact with an otherwise atomized and disengaged public. There is nothing objectionable or unworthy about this motive. The problem is that this policy rarely directs attention to the fundamental social, economic and cultural causes of people's estrangement from many of the key institutions of society. Instead, inclusion is represented primarily as a psychological process of validating people in order to make them feel good. The corollary of this principle is that public bodies, including cultural and educational ones, should do everything possible to avoid undertaking initiatives that may make people feel bad or not even good about themselves. As a result, schools must ensure that their pupils never experience failure or lack affirmation, and that they possess high levels of self-esteem. University lecturers are put under pressure to mark positively, and to provide a climate of support where no undergraduate feels intimidated or offended. Galleries and museums are charged with affirming visitors, and ensuring that they don't feel overwhelmed or daunted by their experience.

In June 2003, Professor Christopher Smout complained about the dumbing down of the National Museums of Scotland. His comment followed a policy statement from six museums, which put historical research at the end of a list of eleven priorities. The response of Gordon Rintoul, Director of the National Museum of Scotland, summed up the approach of the tuned-in cultural mandarin, by indicating that his mission was to expand the museum's learning and events programmes for the public to ensure that 'we fulfil our educational role and provide enjoyment for our visitors'.[10] So the official policy of affirmation is: No to research, yes to fun.

---

[10] Cited in the *Daily Telegraph*, 21 July 2003.

The therapeutics of affirmation that drive the social inclusion agenda is spelled out by Tyne and Wear museums in the following terms:

> Since 1993 several Tyne and Wear museums and galleries have shown community exhibitions chosen and curated by local people. Five main aims underpin these projects: to give people greater confidence in their own ability to assess and to appreciate art, to provide wider access to the gallery collection and a better understanding of how a gallery works, to make visitors aware that art can be interpreted in a variety of different ways and that there is no one right answer, to create an enjoyable and stimulating experience for both participants and gallery visitors, and to focus particularly on people with disabilities and disadvantaged groups as a way of encouraging confidence and self-esteem.[11]

On both sides of the Atlantic, the mission statements of cultural and educational institutions are peppered with references to undertaking the task of encouraging confidence and self-esteem. Unfortunately, the worthy objective of making people feel good about themselves is not always consistent with the genuine demands made on a person by authentic cultural and educational experiences. Trying to make sense of complex ideas and art forms can be at times a dispiriting experience. Such experience necessarily involves the act of discovery – which can be intimidating, frightening and confusing. No wonder that so often we feel very small, disoriented and defensive when confronted with challenging experiences. And often when we do poorly, it is difficult not to feel bad about ourselves.

It is precisely because an intellectual journey involves unexpected tests and challenges that it is ill-suited to the task

[11] See www.culture.gov.uk/pdf/musums.pdf + %22museums + for + the + many %22&hl = en&ieUTF-8.

of providing unquestioned affirmation. That is why the cultural and educational experience dictated by the agenda of social inclusion has little to do with a journey of discovery – and why institutions committed to the policy of social inclusion end up *excluding* challenging experiences from their premises. This process is particularly striking in primary education. Instead of attempting to inspire children through challenging and stretching them, the education system is devoted to making them feel good. The premise of current pedagogy is that children, particularly those who are disadvantaged, need constant affirmation if they are to succeed. 'At some point in the last few decades, the educational world came to agree that its overriding priority was to make children feel good about themselves: none should feel inferior to anyone else or a failure', notes Melanie Phillips.[12] As Phillips notes, ensuring that children possess high self-esteem has become a fundamental premise of the inclusivist agenda.

Concern with raising or maintaining children's self-esteem is based on the assumption that children are far too fragile to deal with being tested and challenged. It is frequently suggested that they need to be insulated from the experience of failure if they are to avoid permanent emotional damage. Inclusion and affirmation are therefore fundamentally at odds with a challenging curriculum that stretches children in order to realize their potential. The education system has become dominated by what US critic Maureen Stout has called The Feel-Good Curriculum, which means that 'teachers lower their expectation of students, which research shows is one of the most damaging things we can do, since students will fulfil our expectations, high or low'.[13]

A preoccupation with children's self-esteem has fostered a preoccupation towards attending to children's emotional needs – often at the expense of intellectual ones. The school is gradually

---

[12] Phillips (1998), p. 12.
[13] Stout (2000), p. 160.

becoming transformed into a clinic. Is it any surprise that the UK-based Mental Health Foundation has recommended that schools should constitute a focal point for mental health intervention? Leading educationalists argue that schools spend too much time promoting intellectual subjects and too little on social and emotional skills. The UK government's advisory group on education for citizenship and the teaching of democracy in schools considers self-esteem an important core skill. The Department for Education's guiding statement on 'sex and relationship' education instructs schools to build pupils' self-esteem. The growing influence of the 'feel-good curriculum' indicates that children's education is increasingly subject to the dictates of the agenda of affirmation through inclusion.

The attempt to insulate children from challenging and painful experiences is often motivated by an understandable desire to protect them from the harsh realities of life. Unfortunately this sentiment has been transformed into an ideology that dictates that those children's feelings must be protected at all costs. As the objective of protecting children's feelings becomes an end in itself, so the pedagogy of praise and affirmation has encouraged intellectual complacency in the schools. There is a systematic attempt to abolish the perception of failure, and children can expect continuous praise and gold stars for their effort. The implicit message transmitted to pupils is that you are judged on effort, rather than what you have achieved. As Stout notes, 'this idea destroys the notion of working toward a goal and thereby undermines the very idea of excellence'.[14]

The reluctance to make value judgements about what children have achieved has been extended to the world of adulthood. There, too, the desire to protect people's feelings is 'judged more important than the desire to stimulate real creativity or instil respect for special achievement'. As John Tusa notes in his essay

---

[14] Stout (2000), p. 163.

'On Creativity', 'in the process of valuing every individual's worth and effort, the definition of creativity was extended so widely that it almost undermined any belief in its true meaning: the exceptional act of imaginative discovery and expression in an art form'.[15] Consequently, the agenda of inclusion through affirmation has a negative impact, not only on children's education, but on intellectual and cultural life in general.

The institutionalization of recognition

The agenda of social inclusion represents an attempt to give meaning to people's lives through providing individuals with a sense of affirmation. It aims to respond to circumstances in which people have lost the web of meaning that would once have enabled them to understand who they are and where they stand in relation to others. However, social inclusion avoids the question of how *communities* can forge a web of meaning through which people can make sense of their lives and ensure that their actions are affirmed. Instead, inclusion is oriented towards the atomized individual, and leaves the big questions in abeyance.

Today's society appears to possess a diminished capacity to answer the question of who we are. One symptom of this trend is the politicization of identities. As the American social commentator Jedediah Purdy has remarked, 'identity politics, based on sex, sexuality, and, mostly, race and ethnicity, suggests that politics should work not so much to give people *things* such as education and jobs as to give them *recognition*'.[16] The growth of identity politics and the consequent demand for recognition has had a significant influence on contemporary political discourse and policy making. The policy of social inclusion

[15] John Tusa, 'On Creativity', in Tusa (2003), p. 6.
[16] Purdy (1999), p. 64.

represents an attempt to respond to this demand, and to cultivate it further.

The reorientation of government towards the project of affirming people is linked to the objective of forging a stable relationship with people in society. This development represents an attempt to confront the problem of legitimation faced by authorities throughout the Western world.[17] Recognition through the institution of the state involves a mix of policies that seek to affirm and validate the individual, and attempting to make people feel good about themselves is a central motif of this process. Therapeutic techniques are employed throughout the public sphere: since the early 1980s, when counselling emerged as a government policy directed at reintegrating the unemployed, therapeutic intervention has become a normal feature of social policy.[18] Moreover, the loss of credibility in the project of classical welfarism has encouraged the state to adopt a more individualized and therapeutic style of policy making. In both the UK and the US, policies are increasingly represented as 'supporting' and 'empowering', if not quite treating, individuals.

Policies developed since the mid-1990s do not aim to 'solve' problems so much as to support otherwise disempowered clients and target groups. This is particularly the case with policies that are designed to tackle social exclusion. The manner in which the language of social exclusion and inclusion is used conveys the impression that people suffer from disadvantage as a psychological condition of their existence. Disadvantage is frequently depicted as the consequence of the absence of affirmation: a state of mind caused by the absence of self-worth. Norman Fairclough's study of the language of New Labour suggests that social exclusion is conceptualized as a 'condition people are in, not something that is done to them. Social exclusion is rarely

---

[17] This point is further explored in Furedi (2003).
[18] See Furedi (2003), chapter 4.

presented as a process but rather something like illness that people suffer from.'[19] It is not so much about poverty or economic disadvantage, but the feeling of not being a part of the important institutions of society. The premise upon which this version of the problem is based is that people become excluded because they lack the sense of self-worth to participate in the institutions of society. That is why institutions need to affirm such individuals if they are to break down the apparent barriers to inclusion.

The experience of social exclusion is frequently presented as a subjective one. 'Social exclusion is perceived and experienced "subjectively"', write the authors of a 1999 report for the Scottish Executive. This report presents social exclusion as a form of social isolation that encompasses 'lack of contact with other people, a feeling of being trapped, low self-esteem and self-confidence, and feelings of insecurity, hopelessness and depression'.[20] The Library and Information Commission's report *Libraries: the essence of inclusion* echoes the same point, indicating that social exclusion is experienced subjectively and is therefore 'specific and relative to each individual, group or environment'.[21] Here the erosion of civic solidarity and informal networks is recast as essentially a psychological problem, to which education and culture are offered as an antidote. The policy of lifelong learning is frequently justified on the grounds that it helps to raise the self-esteem of communities and individuals. As Kathryn Ecclestone notes in her study of lifelong learning: 'ideas about creating "safe spaces", "privileging the learner's voice", and offering people recognition and "positive

---

[19] N. Fairclough, (2000), *New Labour, New Language?*, London: Routledge, pp. 54–5.

[20] William O'Connor and Jane Lewis, 'Experiences of Social Exclusion in Scotland', Scottish Executive. Central Research Unit, Research Programme Research Findings No. 73, 1999.

[21] Library and Information Commission, *Libraries: the essence of inclusion*, 2000.

unconditional regard" ' influence the discussion on this subject. They have led to a focus on 'the psychological and emotional minutiae of people's "fragile learning identities", learning biographies and narratives'.[22] This emphasis on conferring affirmation and recognition tends to subordinate the experience of education to that of treatment – in this case, for life.

The psychological dimension is decisive in the representation of exclusion. The Library and Information Commission explicitly focuses on what it calls the 'psychology of exclusion', noting that 'individuals may become excluded through experiencing or perceiving alienation; isolation; lack of identity; low self-confidence, low self-esteem; passivity; dependence, bewilderment, fear, anger, apathy, low aspirations and hopelessness'.[23] Tackling this psychology of exclusion is not justified simply on the grounds that it assists social integration, but also because managing this condition of psychological distress is interpreted as an integral part of the business of the cultural and educational establishment. Thus inclusion, both at the level of policy making and that of culture, represents an attempt to fulfil the demand for recognition and affirmation

In its most extreme form, the ethos of inclusion subordinates social and cultural policies to the exigencies of recognition and the therapeutic ethos. In the domain of culture, the Department for Culture, Media and Sport (DCMS) has vigorously promoted the inclusion agenda through projects that make people feel good about themselves. It has targeted museums, galleries, cultural organizations like the Arts Council, and local cultural services, to adopt its therapeutic approach. A document published by the DCMS, *Centres for Social Change: Museums, Galleries and Archives for All*, demands that curators of museums and galleries

---

[22] Kathryn Ecclestone, 'Lifelong learning: education or therapy?', *Spiked-online*, 28 January 2003.
[23] Kathryn Ecclestone, 'Lifelong learning: education or therapy?', *Spiked-online*, 28 January 2003.

take on board the objective of 'combating social exclusion', and instructs curators that they have a duty to 'increase individuals' self-worth, value and motivation' and to raise 'self-esteem'.[24] The goal of transforming Britain's cultural institutions into centres for therapeutic engagement with excluded people is one of the clearest illustrations of the project to construct a public infrastructure for the cultivation of a therapeutic ethos. This project represents the most distinctive feature of cultural policy today.

Although the concept of social inclusion is vague, and used to refer to a wide variety of problems, its central focus is to establish a series of linkages between formal institutions and the excluded. Policy statements across government departments continually adopt the rhetoric, and in recent years there has been a systematic attempt to present policies in the sphere of sports, culture and arts from the perspective of inclusion.[25] The Northern Ireland Executive has also adopted this approach. One of its recent consultation papers affirmed the need to help 'increase social inclusion and build self-esteem through participation in culture, arts and leisure activities'.[26]

Government policy and elite interests have always influenced the direction adopted by cultural and educational institutions. However, with the exception of totalitarian regimes, most governments have tended at least to pay lip-service to valuing education and the arts for their own sake. Today, the imperative of social engineering overwhelms such sentiments. Even experts involved in the field of cultural policy have adopted the language of the social engineer, and are likely to adopt arguments such as this:

New confidence and skills; new friendships and social

---

[24] Department of Culture, Media and Sports, *Centres for Social Change: Museums, Galleries and Archives for All.*

[25] Sports Scotland (2000), *Social Inclusion.*

[26] Northern Ireland Executive (2000), *Investing for Health*, Belfast, p. 55.

opportunities; cooperation towards achievement; involvement
in consultation and local democracy; affirmation and questioning of identity; strengthening commitment to place;
intercultural links, positive risk-taking – these ... are crucial
means of fighting social exclusion. Participation in the arts
does this partly by building individual and community
competence, but more importantly by building belief in the
possibility of positive social change.[27]

Here the magical powers assigned to participation in arts appear
as a celebration of culture. But the advocacy of art on the basis of
arguments that have nothing to do with it makes art into an
instrument of therapeutic propaganda. The very use of the term
'participation' indicates that what is at stake is merely the act of
taking part; and since taking part is an end in itself, it matters
little what people participate in. It certainly has little to do with
art or education. Art can be created by artists, and studied,
appreciated or cultivated by others. Education is a process that
involves learning, reflection, imagining and engagement with
ideas. Neither art nor education are experiences like celebrations,
spectacles or elections, in which one participates.

The term participation evokes the spirit of the democratic
ideal. But it is a term that needs to be handled with caution. It
was noted in Chapter 3 that the meaning of participation is
sometimes subverted in the cause of forging an element of
interaction with the electorate. E-voting is a striking example of
how maintaining the illusion of participation has become the
overriding motif. Popular participation is the precondition for
ensuring that people have an opportunity to make choices about
matters that affect their lives, and it is right that people ought to
have a chance to participate in forums that decide how public
money is spent on the arts and education. However, exporting

<hr />

[27]   F. Matarosso, 'Use or Ornament? The Social Impact of Participation in the
Arts', *Comedia*, 1997.

this idea into decision-making about how the arts are run turns the meaning of participation into an empty ritual. 'Cultural inclusion implies allowing people to comment on, even rewrite the stories which museums or others tell us about ourselves' argue advocates of this approach.[28] People are, of course, entitled to rewrite whatever they want, and to transmit their opinions to the cultural elite. The public has an important contribution to make to the world of culture. But whatever contribution it is making, it is not participating in the arts. The public is an audience, at best a critical and educated one. All talk about the 'partnership' between the audience and a cultural institution simply obscures the reality that art is created and produced by artists. Participatory art is nothing more than a public ritual, designed to bind people together through an activity sanctioned by the cultural mandarins. Such activities elevate the taking part and the being there to create the illusion of participation in an activity that actually is beyond the capacity of most of us.

Perpetuating the illusion of participation in art trivializes the artistic experience, and restrains the cultivation of taste and judgement. But its negative consequences pale into insignificance compared to the damage that the promotion of participation in education inflicts on intellectual life. In universities, this process has weakened the line that divides teacher and student. Through the institutionalization of this pseudo-democratic ethos, students are flattered to believe that their view is just as valid as those of their teachers. An environment in which the title 'Teacher' is deprecated and everyone is declared to be a learner, the status of knowledge of a subject is undermined. This caricature of equality between learners undermines the foundation on which the transmission of knowledge can take place. While such an environment may flatter all learners as equal participants in university education, it is at the expense of real learning.

[28] Pachter and Landry (2001), p. 97.

The celebration of ordinariness

It can be argued that the project of transforming culture and education into instruments of recognition does no one any harm. In previous times, the ruling powers have used circuses, spectacles, rituals and religions to make people feel good, so what's wrong with turning schools, universities and museums towards that objective? There are two interrelated problems with the institutionalization of recognition through culture and education. It distracts artistic and intellectual life from developing its vision and ideas; and it encourages the conservative impulse of cultural flattery, instead of challenging the public to aspire to a higher level of achievement.

The policy of inclusion through recognition self-consciously attempts to validate people as they are. 'I don't understand how you can speak to people if you don't celebrate their voices', argues the American populist educator Henry Giroux.[29] Unfortunately, the celebration of people's voices is not always consistent with a serious intellectual or aesthetic experience. Education involves challenging people's perception of themselves, calling into question their common sense, and, at its best, demanding that they become something other than what they once were. The institutionalization of recognition makes no demand on people to adopt an active relationship with culture and education, and it discourages them from learning to distinguish between the ordinary and the exceptional.

In practice, the celebration of people's voices turns into the exaltation of the ordinary. The public is conceived of as consisting of ordinary people, whose ordinariness must be cultivated by institutions of culture and education. In Britain, universities are attempting to create an environment that is not alien to the ordinary undergraduate – instead, it should feel like a

---

[29] Giroux (1992), p. 13.

home away from home. It has been argued that one reason why working-class black youngsters are deterred from applying to Cambridge University is because the city lacks a night life – and so would-be applicants are assured that there is 'plenty of raga, soca and hiphop bands on offer'.[30] In American universities, staff are fully trained in making the ordinary student feel comfortable. Affirmation of the student's voice is a principal theme of the ethos of campus life.

The celebration of ordinariness seeks to endow banality and everyday experience with cultural significance. In a recent exhibition titled 'Telling Lives' at the New York Historical Society, three white-haired ladies sat listening to ordinary people recount their 10-minute stories. After it is finished, a computer prompts the elderly women to tell their stories in front of the camera. According to a review of this exhibition, 'The women are not famous, but they're exactly the reason "Telling Lives" was created.' It appears that recording stories quickly and cheaply provides a large archive of material that can be used in museums and libraries.[31] Talk is not only cheap – it can be readily converted into an object of cultural significance.

Matters are even more complicated when recognition of the ordinary is institutionalized as an automatic right. Recognition as a cultural-political and policy-sanctioned right is consistent with the bureaucratic imperative of treating the individual according to an impersonal general formula. It overlooks individual needs and differences, and fails to distinguish between achievement and failure, wisdom and ignorance. A real recognition of the individual requires that choices are made between knowledge and opinion, and contributions that are worth esteeming and those that are not.

[30] Cited in Claire Fox, 'The Massification of Higher Education', in Hayes and Wynyard (2002), p. 138.
[31] Leslie Kandell, 'Stories of the Things That Mattered to You', *New York Times*, 9 November 2003.

Too often the call to celebrate people's voices serves as a euphemism for dishonest flattery. These days the word 'creative' is routinely used to describe any endeavour undertaken by a human being. Educational and cultural projects seek to reassure potential clients that 'we are all creative' and 'we are all special'. It seems that creativity is a characteristic that we are naturally born with. As Peter Jenkinson, director of Creative Partnership, informed the Museum Association conference in October 2003, 'we are all born 100 per cent creative'. No doubt, words of praise and encouragement are useful in motivating people to engage with new experiences. But when praise and encouragement are institutionalized and spoon-fed in a formulaic manner, they serve to demotivate people from putting themselves to the test. There is a fundamental difference between being open to the idea that individual creativity may be achieved by every person and declaring that we are all creative. The promiscuous designation of the label 'creative' overlooks the fact that achievement involves hard work, painful encounters and personal development. Creativity is not a personal characteristic but the outcome of inspired, hard-earned achievement. That is why most of us are not only not special, but too often do not have the opportunity or the inclination to become special. One of the principal casualties of the politics of recognition is commitment to the notion of intellectual and aesthetic development.

Advocates of the institutionalization of recognition regard the demand that people rise to the occasion and prove worthy of the intellectual or artistic experience they encounter as an unreasonable one. From this perspective, the very attempt to maintain academic standards is dismissed as the inflexible attitude of an elite wedded to its narrow privilege. According to this standpoint:

> The fear of diluting academic standards is bound up with the dominant knowledge-centred paradigm. Traditionally, the task is seen as one of inducting students into a certain kind

of elitist academic culture. As a consequence, the institutions
of higher education have, on the whole, never felt the need to
adapt themselves to students. On the contrary, the assumption
has been that students adapted to them on a 'take it or leave it'
basis.[32]

The demand that universities adapt to the student inexorably
leads to the lowering of expectations. An intellectual challenge by
definition confronts all of us with the ultimatum, 'take it or leave
it'. The attempt to protect students from tackling this challenge
may serve the dogma of inclusion, but only at the expense of
weakening cultural support for intellectual development.

The demand that academic standards should adapt to the
politics of recognition is paralleled in the arts, where policy
makers often stipulate that aesthetic judgements should be
subordinated to the agenda of inclusion. The Runnymede Trust
argues that the issue of cultural recognition – of whose voice is
being heard, and whose representations are being shown – should
predominate over artistic judgements. Aesthetics is seen as a mere
cover for cultural domination. In its report *The Future of Multi-
Ethnic Britain*, the Trust concludes that 'funding and resourcing
policies should consciously attend to issues of cultural recognition, identity and belonging, and therefore question many
customary criteria of quality and aesthetic value'.[33] The report
explicitly acknowledges that what it proposes is 'a major culture
change – indeed, a cultural revolution'.[34] This self-conscious
marginalization of artistic standards and quality highlights the
feeble and philistine foundation on which the policy of
recognition is constructed.

The politics of recognition means accepting as valid people's

[32] Robin Usher, 'Qualification, Paradigms and Experiential Learning in
Higher Education', in Fulton (1989), p. 79.
[33] 'Arts, media and sport', in *The Future of Multi-Ethnic Britain*, 2000, p. 160.
[34] 'Arts, media and sport', in *The Future of Multi-Ethnic Britain*, 2000, p. 166.

accounts of their subjective states. This reluctance to question people's accounts of themselves is reflected by the current climate of cultural relativism. However, the absence of a common moral grammar gives recognition a superficial and provisional character. Recognition without dialogue and critical engagement represents a form of self-validation that tends to promote unstable and defensive identities. Automatic recognition provided by institutions as a matter of routine fails to engage with people's desire to be valued. But by treating recognition as a right formally granted through an institution, it creates a demand for even more guarantees for affirmation.

Recognition accorded through the institutionalization of inclusion represents the cultural flattery of passive subjectivity. Ironically, the institutionalization of the right to recognition necessarily leads to emptying it of any moral content. Recognition that means something to the individual is linked to the sense of achievement. Such a right can never satisfy the craving to be recognized – it merely incites the individual to demand more assurances of respect. But the very act of offering respect to those who crave it may make matters more complicated. As Richard Sennett suggests, the weak may quite rightly experience the extension of such respect as an empty gesture or, worse still, as a ritual confirming their position of inferiority.[35] The celebration of the ordinary rarely succeeds in enthusing its audience. But the problem with the culture of flattery is not simply that it doesn't work. It continually transmits powerful signals that undermine the foundation on which cultural and intellectual life can thrive. Instead of promoting public engagement with the sphere of ideas, it reinforces people's estrangement from this realm.

[35] Sennett (2003).

6   Treating People as Children

Projects collecting oral histories, individual stories, university seminars devoted to undergraduates talking about what's relevant to them, and community exhibitions of people's favourite things are the kind of experiences celebrated by the cult of the ordinary. This celebration of the ordinary is often presented as a democratic, anti-elitist affirmation of the people. This chapter suggests that it is none of that. What it reveals is the patronizing assumptions of the elites that manage institutions of culture and education. Such sentiments are particularly conspicuous in the media, where programmers genuinely believe that ordinary folk have an attention span of three seconds. On both sides of the Atlantic, news organizations searching for the elusive youth market are transforming current events programmes into racy spectacles fit for six-year-olds. Some television broadcasters have expressed alarm at the diminishing quality of their product. Just before his death in the summer of 2003, the veteran newscaster David Brinkley said of the medium that was his life: 'television news has become so trivial and devoid of content as to be little different from entertainment programming'.

Criticism of the direction adopted by the media is invariably dismissed as the knee-jerk reaction of elitist and anti-democratic old fogies who are addicted to the high-brow. But it is not the true spirit of democracy that encourages spoon-feeding culture. The policies of inclusion and affirmation rarely translate into an authentic respect for the wisdom possessed by the intelligent public. It is precisely because the cultural elite has no real respect for people's capacity to improve themselves and to rise to the challenge of the opportunities provided by education and culture that it tends to treat them as potential patients rather than as an audience for ideas. Immunizing school children, university students or museum-goers from feeling intimidated and demoralized might seem an enlightened policy of support. However, by treating people as weak and vulnerable individuals who are likely to stumble when confronted by an intellectual challenge, such cultural attitudes serve to create a climate of low expectations.

Low expectations reveal contempt for those ordinary people who are the target of cultural and educational institutions. As the poet Nicholas Murray asks: 'Does respect for an audience involve appealing to the lowest common denominator, the least demanding performance, the most untaxing pleasure, or does it mean crediting the common reader, the concert goer, the civilised citizen, with some intelligence and appetite for invigorating artistic experience?'[1] A similar question can be posed in relation to the attitude that educational institutions have adopted towards students. Even elite institutions like Harvard University are busy creating an environment where students are treated as fragile children that need to be protected from the risks posed by intellectual disputes and conflict. According to Dorothy Rabinowitz, 'first-year law students can hardly fail to notice the pall of official disapproval now settled over everything smacking of conflict and argument'.[2] A new programme designed for first-year students, 'Managing Difficult Conversations', instructs students on the need to acknowledge emotions in their verbal communication. A publication written by this programme's authors explains in capitals that 'A Difficult Conversation is Anything You Find It Hard to Talk About'. The programme not

[1]   Nicholas Murray, 'Culture and Accessibility', in Wallinger and Warnock (2000), pp. 58–9.
[2]   See Dorothy Rabinowitz, 'Difficult Conversations', *The Wall Street Journal*, 19 November 2002.

only infantilizes university students, but also minimizes the role of reason and logic in intellectual debate. It appears that in a 'difficult conversation', which is anything that a person finds hard to talk about, 'logic/reason' has to be combined with 'emotions and personal experience'. If even an elite university like Harvard adopts the mission of instructing young people how to talk about their feelings and experiences, it is not surprising that the more ordinary ones routinely treat their students as confused children.

Infantilized culture

No one actually explicitly supports the process of dumbing down. When institutions adopt a cavalier attitude towards standards they do not do so on the grounds that they want to provide the public with an inferior education or undemanding cultural experience. They do so because they believe that people will feel alienated unless they engage with experiences that are deemed to be directly relevant to their lives and linked to their personal experiences. But inevitably, this emphasis on relevance exists in a state of permanent tension with the acquisition of objective knowledge and an artistic sensibility. Powerful ideas often have an abstract character and are developed through the assimilation of a range of conflicting experiences. That is why they often appear so much at odds with everyday common sense and with the insights gained through personal experience. Acquiring objective knowledge cannot be confined to the process of reflecting on an individual's life story. It also requires a form of education that distances the student from the immediate and everyday, so as to stimulate the mind to imagine other possibilities. There is no direct route from personal emotions to objective knowledge, and students need to be confronted with worlds that are 'irrelevant' to their lives. Sometimes they even have to understand that the knowledge they gained through life is quite irrelevant to their ability to grasp a particular subject.

At some point law students at Harvard will find that acknowledging their emotional and personal experience is not what legal training is about. Studying law requires an under-standing of objective facts and their interpretation through forms of reasoning that have little to do with personal experience. It could be argued that the therapeutic encouragement that Harvard students receive need not prevent them from becoming brilliant legal scholars. However, its privileging of the status of personal experience compromises the intellectual horizons of its students. This process can be seen even more clearly in relation to children's education. A recent study of US publishers' guidelines to authors of schoolbook texts makes frightening reading. Guided by the imperative of relevance, these instructions seek to protect children from any references that are remotely distant from their experience. For example, the guidelines advise that a story set in the mountains discriminates against students from flatlands; and one story of a blind mountaineer who climbed to the top of Mount McKinley, the highest peak in North America, was rejected 12-11 by the panel vetting it because of 'regional bias'. It is felt that children should not be expected to read or comprehend stories set in an unfamiliar terrain. Diane Ravitch, the author of this study, notes:

> Consider the impoverishment of imagination that flows from such assumptions: *No reading passage on a test may have a specific geographical setting*: every event should occur in a generic locale. Under these assumptions, no child should be expected to understand a story set in a locale other than the one that he or she currently lives in or a locale that *has no distinguishing characteristics*.[3]

---

[3]   Ravitch (2003), p. 10.

The key point that comes across from Ravitch's text is that the more that school texts have to meet the criterion of relevance, the greater their cultural content is diminished.

The instruction that children living in Switzerland ought not be tested about stories set in a Newfoundland fishing village, or that Asian students should not be examined about stories located in New York, may strike many as a grotesque caricature of an otherwise sound policy of cultural sensitivity. However, most of the more routine policies associated with the ethos of access and relevance are premised upon the same assumptions that have been internalized by the zealous overseers of children's textbooks. From the infant school right through to the university and the museum, the public is continually expected to founder and crumble when entering a cultural terrain that is distant from its own life. Even textbooks targeting university students make an effort to imitate publications aimed at secondary school students: as the content of university courses become more relevant, it has also become less theoretical and less abstract.

The unintended consequence of Harvard University's course on Managing Difficult Conversations, or the publishers' guidelines on school texts, is to infantilize cultural and intellectual life. The significance such initiatives attach to the appearance of relevance and to direct personal experience tends to diminish their intellectual content. At their worst, institutions peddling relevance turn public education and arts into a form of individual therapy that simply affirms rather than teaches or stimulates. Such initiatives are often presented as reflecting a shift towards a more democratic attitude towards culture. They are meant to increase 'participation', 'widen access', 'empower communities', 'break down barriers' and give people an opportunity to express their 'voice'. However these initiatives have little to do with the democratization process. Projects devoted to a more democratic orientation would seek to educate the public to develop its understanding of new and challenging encounters. Instead, these initiatives hope to expand participation by eliminating such challenging encounters, in an attempt to prevent people from being put off by them. As Josie Appleton argues, 'when the new cultural elite talks about breaking down the barriers of culture, in practice this means the reduction of cultural experience to an instant, emotional connection'.[4] She adds that 'reflection and judgment are seen as exclusive, as blocking the connection and shutting people out'.

The infantilization of culture assumes its most distinct character in its elevation of personal experience. When education and culture is treated as the projection of personal sentiment, ideas and objects of art become valued because of their meaning to the individual rather than because of the achievement and importance they represent to the public. A culture that exists in order to help people find themselves fosters a mood of self-obsession and inward orientation. 'This represents a regression to a childlike state, where there is no distinction made between what is of value to me and what is of general value,' notes Appleton.[5] Children tend to value what directly gives them pleasure and affirmation. Cultivating such attitudes amongst the public represents its infantilization. The celebration of the ordinary voice, through the idea that 'this is my story', is not a million miles away from the emotional sentiment that cries out 'this is my toy'.

Infantilizing people

The policies associated with social inclusion and access are based upon a uniquely feeble version of the human subject. In the imagination of the cultural and educational mandarin, the public

[4]   Josie Appleton, 'Infantilising Art', forthcoming.
[5]   Josie Appleton, 'Infantilising Art', forthcoming.

lacks the resources to engage with difficult intellectual or artistic encounters, and people are assumed to be incapable of rising to the occasion and overcoming the obstacles they meet. This view transmits the perception that people are children who need to have their hands held as they enter a university campus or pass through the door of a museum or a public library. But the systematic transmission of the idea that people cannot possibly cope when confronted with an intellectual or artistic challenge can have a damaging impact on the public imagination. It is not yet the case that people entering the Metropolitan Museum or the V&A are offered counselling to deal with the intimidating surroundings in which exhibitions are held – however, a young adult becoming a university undergraduate or postgraduate can now access a variety of therapeutic services to help him or her come to terms with the trauma of campus life.

Students confronted with the ordinary troubles of life are routinely advised to seek professional advice and counselling. A change in individual circumstance is often elevated into a problem that requires professional support. Transition counsellors specialize in offering support to individuals embarking on a new phase in their lives. 'The counselling team are fully aware of the importance of managing transition and are here to help you find the way ahead', acclaims the University of Bath Counselling Service on its website. As illustrations of the kind of the transitions that might require professional support, the service mentions entering university as a first-year undergraduate, the move of second-year students from campus-based residence to living in town, final-year students returning after being away on placement, and newly arrived postgraduate students. 'It could be that feelings of self-confidence are quite threatened by the unfamiliarity of new surroundings and new people', warns the service.

Academics too are expected to treat undergraduates as children rather than young men and women. They face continuous pressure to minimize the demands they place on students. In Britain and in the US, university students are often not expected to be able to possess an understanding of grammatical rules or the ability to write an essay. The American Conference for College Composition and Communication, the body that represents professional teachers of this subject, believes that 'if we can convince our students that spelling, punctuation, and usage are less important than content, we [will] have removed a major obstacle in their developing their ability to write'.[6] The exhortation to remove the barriers posed by spelling, punctuation and usage illustrates the kind of education that the access agenda offers to the ordinary student. It is a form of education that is more interested in giving students a sense of achievement than in educating them.

The art of patronizing students is often defined as 'best practice' in universities. Lecturers are required to provide undergraduates with course material that leaves little to chance. The relatively informal student–teacher relationship has been turned into a contractual one. A course outline and reading list is increasingly regarded as a contract that obliges the academic to deliver clearly outlined learning objectives. Students are given handouts to explain what the lecturer is doing. They are frequently provided with lecture notes and with model exam papers that explain how students should answer questions. Lecturers are trained to avoid forms of behaviour that might hurt a student's feelings. Feedback must always be supportive, students should never be told that they are wrong, and examiners must always attempt to find and say something positive about an essay. The style of affirmation favoured by parenting experts for infants has been adopted by the university. Inevitably, the more energy that academics devote to attend to the emotional needs of

---

6   Cited in Thomas F. Bertonneau (1996), *Declining Standards at Michigan Public Universities*. Midland, MI: Mackinac Center for Public Policy.

their undergraduates, the less seriously they take them as potential intellectuals.

This process of infantilization expresses a pessimistic and anti-democratic account of people. The target audience of policies of inclusion consists of individuals who bear no resemblance to the ideal of the democratic subject. Ideals of democratic participation presuppose citizens who possess the intelligence and responsibility to act autonomously and exercise their rights. They are able to criticize and take criticism. They possess maturity, a sense of responsibility and are prepared to take an interest in matters that affect not only them but also other sections of their community. Contemporary cultural and educational institutions transmit signals that indicate that people are not expected to behave in accordance with democratic ideals. Instead, they expect their audience to be emotional, only interested in themselves, lacking in curiosity and immature.

Inverted snobbery

From the perspective of our cultural mandarins, anxiety about the intellectual crisis facing the university, the process of dumbing down or the infantilization of the public are entirely misplaced. They believe that all that has happened is that education and culture have become more inclusive, and they interpret the developments criticized in this book as the positive outcome of policies promoting the democratization of culture. As a concept, inclusiveness is presented as an expression of impulses that are anti-elitist and participatory. Hostility to *elitism* is now mandatory for any individual who hopes to join the cultural elite. And the meaning of the term elitist has been expanded to describe language usage, education and cultural experience that is not deemed to be directly relevant or accessible to ordinary people. The language of populism that informs cultural life is informed by a sensibility that regards claims to artistic and intellectual superiority with cynicism. The description of an institution as an elitist one usually contains the sense of disapproval and condemnation. When Oxford or Cambridge are described in such terms, no one is left in any doubt that these are institutions of privilege, dominated by an old-boy network who are out of touch with the aspirations of ordinary folk. The Opera House in Covent Garden symbolizes everything that is said to be wrong with elitist institutions. It is stuffy, expensive, irrelevant and exclusive, and its productions do little to affirm the lives of people living in inner-city London. Worse still, it demands that the audience listens and concentrates for long periods of time to music and songs that are not part of their daily life.

There is of course a sound argument to be made about ensuring that people can afford the price of a ticket to the opera. But criticisms of the opera are not confined to its pricing policy. They express hostility toward the opera as an art form on the grounds that it only engages with the taste of a small elite of privileged men and women. Calls to redirect expenditure on opera to regional theatres or community art centres are often linked to expressions of cultural preference. The supposedly bold and innovative productions of a community interactive theatre are favourably contrasted to the allegedly lifeless and irrelevant opera patronized by the privileged elite. The language of philistinism employed in such debates has led one commentator to write about today's 'elite of anti-elitists'.[7]

It is important to realize that the institutionalization of anti-elitist sentiment is not a response to the assertion of popular culture from below. It is not ordinary folk who are in the vanguard of the campaign to transform education and culture to one that is deemed accessible and relevant. Anti-elitism is a cause that has emerged from within the elite itself. It can be most

[7]   Walden (2001), p. 43.

usefully seen as a form of snobbishness – or, more precisely, as inverted snobbery.

A snob is traditionally defined as one whose ideas and conduct are prompted by vulgar admiration for wealth and social position. Inverted snobbery is motivated by an uncritical embrace of the ordinary and the popular. Inverted snobs are uncritically critical of forms of culture that were valued and cultivated in the past. What they object to is not the aesthetic content of a particular art form, but the fact that it is old and was produced or appreciated by the wrong type of people. The main targets of inverted snobs are the elites who are still self-consciously elitist, and their elitism is regarded as a sin with unpardonable consequences. This is a very different critique of elitism than that which was mounted by progressive movements in the past. The target of nineteenth- and twentieth-century progressive movements was elite privilege and the determination of the oligarchy to control and monopolize society's resources at the expense of the quality of life of the majority. Anti-elitism today is rarely focused on economic power. Rather, its fire is directed against forms of behaviour, culture and education that are often wrongly associated with the elite. Sophisticated language, complex ideas, challenging education, and demanding art forms are today stigmatized as elitist and therefore deemed to be a bad thing. The very claim to standards of excellence can be represented as elitist since, by implication, it disrespects those whose achievements fail to match it. Protecting people from elitist culture is seen as mandatory, since such culture is seen as a threat to the self-esteem of ordinary people.

The anti-elitist stance of the elites has had a profound impact on intellectual life. These attitudes have distracted intellectuals and cultural producers from developing their work in directions that are not directly relevant to the demands of everyday routine. Although intellectuals and artists do their best to develop their work, they continually face institutional pressure to fall in line with current policies. Political compulsion and calculations have always represented a challenge for genuine intellectual work or artistic endeavour. The current era is no exception to this trend. Today there is great pressure upon academics, educators and cultural producers to buy into the populist dogma that has been constructed by anti-elitist elites. As one proponent of the populist turn argues, 'today, a code of intellectual activism which is not grounded in the vernacular of information technology and the discourses and images of popular commercial culture is likely to be ineffective'.[8]

The different manifestations of inverted snobbery often appear as an affectation adopted by a manipulative elite. It is certainly difficult to take powerful and wealthy cultural mandarins seriously when they argue the case for eliminating elitist privilege and extending the agenda of inclusion. Some commentators take the view that the elites do not really mean what they say in relation to culture and education. This standpoint is forcibly argued by the transatlantic critic Christopher Hitchens, who believes that 'populism' has become 'the main tactical weapon, the main vernacular of elitism'. He adds that 'certainly the most successful elitist in American culture now, American politics, is the most successful inventor or manipulator, or leader of populism'.[9]

Hitchens is right to alert us to the top-down character of populist trends in contemporary culture. But the anti-elitism of the cultural elite is not simply an affectation adopted for the purposes of public consumption. It reflects genuine sentiments of an elite that lacks conviction about its own status and authority. When privileged white men who run American universities, or British mandarins who manage the BBC, disparage dead white

---

[8]   Ross (1989), p. 212
[9]   See Christopher Hitchens, 'The Future of the Public Intellectual', *The Nation*, 12 February 2001.

men they are semi-consciously expressing their own contempt for their own personal positions. When graduates of Harvard and Oxford denounce elitist educational institutions they reveal a profound sense of unease about transmitting to society the values that they had internalized in their youth. Unable to rest their authority on the institutions and conventions that have secured their position, they are in the business of searching for an alternative source of legitimacy. In a sense, they have become estranged from the institutions and values that provided the platform on which they built their careers.

The lack of affirmation for the elite's authority has led to a situation where the elite finds it difficult to summon up conviction in its own mission. It does not possess any strong beliefs, and therefore is open to negotiation about what should be valued and ought to be rejected. It has sought to overcome the dilemma posed by its own crisis of belief by declaring that no beliefs can claim to possess a monopoly on truth. That is why the cultural elite is so susceptible to the influence of cultural relativism. Its estrangement from a sense of mission and lack of clarity about truth with a capital T has encouraged a flexible attitude toward values and truth. By putting a question mark against all previously held values and institutions, the elite avoids the necessity of coming up with the answers about what beliefs and practices society ought to value and uphold. Instead of giving answers, it provides recognition and affirmation. The populist policies of inclusion and affirmation help the elite to evade replying to questions for which it has no unambiguous answers.

The elite's loss of conviction in its own authority is most strikingly reflected in the sphere of politics. But it has also had a formidable impact on culture and education. It has helped fuel a process of disorientation, which has undermined the elite's capacity to transmit a clear vision of its objectives. Policy makers, museum directors and university administrators are genuinely uncertain about standards and dubious about the value of maintaining them. Not only are they unwilling to affirm their cultural legacy – they also find it difficult to discriminate between the quality and value of popular entertainment and ideas and works that are the products of genuine intellectual innovation and artistic creativity.

What we have is a disoriented cultural elite that lacks firm convictions and feels unable to project a coherent picture of the world to the rest of society. It is an elite that feels uncomfortable with the idea of self-consciously acting as an elite. Aware of its own incoherence as a group, it does not dare claim to possess attributes of distinctiveness and superiority. Unable to assert itself as a cultural elite, it declares that, in any case, it is wrong to try to improve and educate people; and that not only does it have nothing to teach but it also has a lot to learn from ordinary folk. This apparent reversal of the relationship between elite and people is clearly expressed through the process of inverted snobbery. It is important to underline the word 'apparent' because its current embrace of the people coincides with belief that the public is incapable of engaging with demanding intellectual and cultural encounters. Hence the paradoxical situation in which the celebration of the ordinary coexists with a lack of belief in the capacity of the public to handle sophisticated and complex ideas.

The low expectations that society's institutions have adopted towards the public is a unique feature of our times. Historically, the attitude of the elites towards the public has undergone a number of significant changes.

In pre-modern times, the elites took the view that the public was not capable of understanding Truth and lacked the capacity to grasp profound insights. The opinion of Plato's Socrates that 'it is impossible that a multitude be philosophic' was rarely challenged by the intellectuals of antiquity and pre-modern times. One of the important legacies of the Enlightenment was to challenge this representation of the public. The majority of Enlightenment thinkers continued to have a low opinion of the intellectual capacity of the public to reason, and believed that the ability to think scientifically was confined to members of the elite. However, these thinkers also took the view that it was possible to educate and gradually enlighten the multitudes. From the middle of the nineteenth century, the belief that the elite had a duty to enlighten the people gained strength. This was a project readily embraced by the modern intellectual, and continued to motivate the cultural elites until the 1970s.

One of the distinctive features of the contemporary so-called postmodern era is the loss of conviction in the idea that the public is capable of being enlightened. But scepticism about the project of public enlightenment is rarely expressed in a coherent and explicit form. In an era of inclusion and participation, doubts about the capacity of people cannot be raised in a clear and open manner. We live in an era where clear statements about people's ability are obfuscated by a vocabulary that relies on terms like 'special needs students', 'differently abled people', 'non-traditional students', and 'the intellectually challenged'. This confusing language coexists with the rhetoric of flattery that declares that everyone is special and creative. But at a time when normal university students are routinely described as vulnerable, it is evident that the mental capacity of the public is not held in high esteem.

The flattery of people allows the cultural elite to avoid assuming its traditional role toward the public. Since people are apparently so creative and their ordinary lives provide so many important insights, it would be pointless and arrogant for an elite to assume the burden of enlightening the public. Instead of cultivating the public imagination, the role of the cultural elite becomes to validate and celebrate it. The policy of recognition allows the Establishment to forge a point of contact with people, and also to avoid confronting the crisis of its legitimacy.

The contradictory relationship of today's cultural elite to the public is resolved through the argument that there is something inherently wrong in teaching, instructing or cultivating the taste of the public. This sentiment has acquired the status of an incontrovertible truth among opinion-makers. A report written for the British Arts Council expressed the argument in the following terms:

> Too often in the past, the arts have taken a patronizing attitude to audiences. Too often artists and performers have continued to ply their trade to the same white, middle-class audience. In the back of their minds lurks the vague hope that one day enlightenment might descend semi-miraculously upon the rest, that the masses might get wise to their brilliance.[10]

Under the guise of condemning elitism, the report questions the very idea that artists or intellectuals can have a role in enlightening people. According to this cynical view, the public has little to learn and institutions of culture should get into the business of recognizing this fact.

The construction of a docile public

The cumulative impact of the politics of recognition is the construction of a docile and conformist public. Institutions of culture and education treat the people as consumers who have culture and education spoon-fed to them. The cultural regime of low expectations does little to stimulate public discussion and debate. And in any case, the diminished importance attached to ideas and scepticism towards the status of knowledge means that there is little point in taking such debates too seriously. The absence of culturally affirmed standards deprives people of a common language through which they can make judgements of value and gain coherence as a public. Debate and rational

---

[10] Cited in Walden (2001), p. 108.

argument over the vital issues of the day is difficult in a society that is devoted to the celebration of individual voices.

An intelligent public is the product of intellectual and cultural ferment and intense debate. As the American sociologist C. Wright Mills has argued, the public is distinguished by its ability to develop its arguments and to express them in society. 'In a *public* as I understand the term, virtually as many people express opinions as receive them; public communications are so organised that there is a chance immediately and effectively to answer back to any opinion expressed in public,' observes Wright Mills.[11] Wright Mills places particular emphasis on autonomy and independence from official institutions as one of the preconditions for the functioning of a flourishing public, and has clearly counterposed a public which is 'more or less autonomous in its operation' to what he called *the mass*. In a mass, far fewer people express theirs opinion than receive them. Communications are organized in such a manner that it is difficult for people to 'answer back or with effect'. Most important of all, 'the mass has no autonomy from institutions; on the contrary, agents of authorized institutions interpenetrate this mass, reducing any autonomy it may have in the formation of opinion by discussion'.[12]

Today's cultural climate is more hospitable to the development of a mass than to a public. Argument and debate are often represented as adversarial and damaging. The growth of scepticism and of cultural relativism calls into question the value of battling over ideas. When there is little at stake, debate may seem pointless. But probably the most significant development that serves to undermine the workings of the public is the expansion of official and semi-official institutions into cultural

[11] C. Wright Mills, 'Mass Society and Liberal Education', in Horowitz (1963), p. 355.

[12] C. Wright Mills, 'Mass Society and Liberal Education', in Horowitz (1963), p. 355.

and intellectual life. The massive expansion of the university, the rise of credentialism and the growing intervention of the state in cultural life have reduced the terrain on which the public can exercise its autonomy. Policies which fly the flags of inclusion, access and participation often lead to the penetration of official institutions into people's lives. The auditing of cultural institutions and of the relationship between students and academics tends to compromise informal and spontaneous interaction. Through a variety of devices – lifelong learning, certificates of competence, training and development – people's intellectual and cultural life becomes subject to institutional expectations. These trends stimulate a mood of conformism and passivity.

The imperative of social engineering leads to the colonization of people's informal lives. The accreditation of prior learning is presented as an acknowledgement of the important learning experiences that people have acquired through their encounters in their communities and at work. And many people are delighted that their lives are taken seriously by educators. At a recent academic conference, one woman reported just how pleased she was that her previous life as a housewife was accredited and deemed as relevant to her course. But do we really want our lives to be accredited and certificated by an institution? The formalization of personal experience through institutional recognition has a corrosive impact on the public, and inevitably weakens its autonomy. Accreditation leads to the auditing of personal experience according to criteria established by an external institution. It always contains the potential for forcing the public into a relationship of subservience to the auditors.

The social engineering agenda self-consciously seeks to colonize the life-world of the public. For example, a report written to justify the merits of small museums claims that the strength of small museums lies in 'terms of the impact they can have on individuals and to a lesser extent, whole communities (e.g. enhancing self-esteem, skills development, recuperative

benefits)'. Why? Because they can forge more 'intimate relationships with individual community members' and assist 'the
creation of networks of friends and other social contacts for
elderly people'.[13] Invading the sphere of informal relations is one
of the desired outcomes of this project.

Final thoughts

The trivialization of the public's cultural potential has important
implications for the future of intellectual thought. Intellectuals
need an intelligent public and artists need an engaged critical
audience. Unfortunately, the politics of cultural flattery create
little incentive for people to rise to the occasion. As a result, the
pool of society's creative energy is wasted on creating and
responding to the demand for recognition. Those who insist on
undertaking a genuine journey of intellectual discovery risk being
labelled as elitist and irrelevant. 'I've increasingly become
convinced that in order to be any kind of a public intellectual
commentator or combatant, one has to be unafraid of the charges
of elitism,' writes Christopher Hitchens.[14] Anyone who is
genuinely concerned with the disturbing influences that dominate
our cultural life would find it difficult to disagree with Hitchens's
sentiment.

Intellectuals inside and outside the university, and their
colleagues in the world of culture and the arts, must face up to
the uncomfortable truth that they risk making themselves
irrelevant if they allow current institutional pressures to dominate
their work. Some of us have actively internalized the politics of
cultural flattery while others have sought an easy life by

[13] See *www.resource.gov.uk/documents/lat325* v2.pdf.
[14] See Christopher Hitchens, 'The Future of the Public Intellectual', *The
Nation*, 12 February 2001.

acquiescing in institutional demands. Intellectuals need to reconstitute themselves through reclaiming the autonomy for which their predecessors fought in previous times. Such autonomy can best be constructed by engaging with the public's own aspiration to be taken seriously, and helping to cultivate that aspiration. In an era of the infantilization of culture, treating people as grown-ups has become one of the principal duties of the humanist intellectual.

A lot has been said about the corrosive impact of cultural policies, particularly those of social inclusion, on the quality of contemporary intellectual life. But it would be wrong to put the blame entirely upon governments and cultural institutions. Politicians and public institutions have always attempted to impose their agenda on culture and education, and elected representatives have every right to be interested in the workings of publicly funded institutions. What is worrying is not the role of the political class so much as the compliance of the world of art and education with a philistine social engineering agenda. Nor has all the pressure towards dumbing down come from outside the academy or the arts. The culture of flattery has for long been internalized by educators and cultural producers. Relativist epistemologies and contempt for standards have been endowed with intellectual credibility by academic practitioners. So there do not appear to be many obvious candidates who come out well from this story.

In as much as it means anything, dumbing down does not refer to the intelligence of people. Rather it is a statement about culture – more specifically, about the elites who influence and regulate the flow of cultural ideas. There is very little that we can do to force the elites to give up their instrumentalist and philistine world view. But we can wage a battle of ideas for the hearts and minds of the public. How we do it is one of the key questions of our time.

Bibliography

Alexander, J. C. and Sztompka, P. (eds) (1990) *Rethinking Progress.* Boston, MA: Unwin Hyman.

Appleton, J. (2001) *Museums for 'The People'?* London: Academy of Ideas.

Arendt, H. (1993) *Between Past and Future.* New York: Penguin.

Barnett, R. (1990) *The Idea of Higher Education.* Buckingham: Open University Press.

Bauman, Z. (1987) *Legislators and Interpreters: On Modernity, Postmodernity and Intellectuals.* Cambridge: Polity Press.

Bauman, Z. (1991) *Modernity and the Holocaust.* Cambridge: Polity Press.

Beck, U. (1992) *Risk Society: Towards a New Modernity.* London: Sage.

Beck, U., Giddens, A. and Lash, S. (eds) (1994) *Reflexive Modernisation: Politics, Tradition and Aesthetics in the Modern Social Order.* Cambridge: Polity Press.

Benda, J. (1959) *The Betrayal of the Intellectuals.* Boston, MA: The Beacon Press.

Berman, M. (2001) *The Twilight of American Culture.* New York: Norton.

Berube, M. (1994) *Public Access: Literary Theory and American Cultural Politics.* London: Verso.

Bourdieu, P. (1988) *Homo Academicus.* Cambridge: Polity Press.

Coser, L. A. (1965) *Men of Ideas: A Sociologist's View.* New York: The Free Press.

Cowen, T. (2000) *In Praise of Commercial Culture.* Cambridge, MA: Harvard University Press.

Debray, R. (1981) *Teachers, Writers, Celebrities; The Intellectuals of Modern France.* London: Verso.

Department of Culture, Media and Sport (2000) *Centres For Social Change: Museums, Galleries and Archives for All. Policy guidance on social inclusion for DCMS funded and local authority museums, galleries and archives in England.* London: DCMS.

Eyerman, R. (1994) *Between Culture and Politics; Intellectuals in Modern Society.* Cambridge: Polity Press.

Eyerman, R., Svensson, L. G. and Soderqvist, T. (eds) (1987) *Intellectuals, Universities, and the State in Western Modern Societies.* Berkeley, CA: University of California Press.

Fairclough, N. (2000) *New Labour, New Language?* London: Routledge.

Fink, L., Leonard, S. T. and Reid, D. M. (eds) (1996) *Intellectuals and Public Life; Between Radicalism and Reform.* Ithaca, NY: Cornell University Press.

Fulton, O. (ed.) (1989) *Access and Institutional Change.* Milton Keynes: Open University Press.

Furedi, F. (1992) *Mythical Past, Elusive Future; History and Society in an Anxious Age.* London: Pluto Press.

Furedi, F. (2003) *Therapy Culture: Cultivating Vulnerability in an Anxious Age.* London: Routledge.

Gagnon, A. G. (1987) *Intellectuals in Liberal Democracies; Political Influence and Social Involvement.* New York: Praeger.

Gerth, H. H. and Wright Mills, C. (1958) *From Max Weber: Essays in Sociology.* New York: Oxford University Press.

Giner, S. (1976) *Mass Society.* London: Martin Robertson.

Giroux, H. (1992) *Border Crossings: Cultural Workers and the Politics Of Education.* London: Routledge.

Gouldner, A. W. (1979) *The Future of Intellectuals and the Rise of the New Class.* London: Macmillan Press.

Graham, G. (2002) *Universities: The Recovery of an Idea.* Thorverton: Imprint Academic.

Halsey, A. H. (1992) *Decline of Donnish Dominion: The British Academic Professions in the Twentieth Century.* Oxford: Clarendon Press.

Hayek, F. A. (ed.) (1954) *Capitalism and the Historians.* London: Routledge & Kegan Paul.

Hayek, F. A. (1978) *Three Sources of Human Values.* London: London School of Economics.

Hayes, D. and Wynyard, R. (eds) (2002) *The McDonaldization of Higher Education.* Westport, CT: Bergin & Harvey.

Horowitz, I. L. (ed.) (1963) *Power, Politics and People: The Collected Essays of C. Wright Mills*. London: Oxford University Press.

Huszar, De G. B. (ed.) (1960) *The Intellectuals: A Controversial Portrait*. Glencoe: The Free Press.

Illich, I., Zola, K. I., McKnight, R., Caplan, J. and Shaiken, H. (1977) *Disabling Professions*. New York: Marion Boyars.

Jacoby, R. (1987) *The Last Intellectuals; American Culture in the Age of Academe*. New York: Basic Books.

Jowell, R., Curtice, J., Park, A. *et al.* (eds) (1995) *British Social Attitudes: The 12th Report*. Dartmouth: SCPR.

Koestler, A. (1983) *The Yogi and the Commissar and Other Essays*. London: Hutchinson.

Lasch, C. (1966) *The New Radicalism In America [1889–1963]: The Intellectual as a Social Type*. London: Chatto & Windus.

Leavis, F. R. (1965) *Educations and the University: A Sketch for an English School*. London: Chatto & Windus.

Leavis, Q. D. (1968) *Fiction and the Reading Public*. London: Chatto & Windus.

Lipset, S. M. (1960) *Political Man*. London: Mercury Books.

Luhman, N. (1993) *Risk: A Sociological Theory*. New York: Walter de Gruyter.

Lyotard, J.-F. (1984) *The Postmodern Condition: A report on knowledge*. Minneapolis: University of Minnesota Press.

Mackenzie, G. and Labiner, J. (2002) *Opportunity Lost: The Decline of Trust and Confidence in Government after September 11*. Washington DC: Center for Public Services.

Matarosso, F. (1997) *The Social Impact of Participation in the Arts*. London: Comedia.

Mattick Jr, P. (1986) *Social Knowledge: An Essay on the Nature and Limits of Social Science*. London: Hutchinson.

Melzer, A. M., Weinberger, J. and Zinman, M. R. (2003) *The Public Intellectual: Between Philosophy and Politics*. Lanham, NJ: Rowman & Littlefield.

Michael, J. (2000) *Anxious Intellects: Academic Professionals, Public Intellectuals and Enlightenment Values*. Durham, NC: Duke University Press.

Minihan, J. (2001) *The Nationalisation of Culture*. London: Hamish Hamilton.

Novick, P. (1988) *That Noble Dream: 'The Objectivity Question' and the American Historical Profession*. Cambridge: Cambridge University Press.

Orwell, G. (1941) *The Lion and the Unicorn*. London: Secker & Warburg.

Pachter, M. and Landry, C. (2001) *Culture at the Crossroads; Culture and Cultural Institutions at the beginning of the 21st Century*. London: Comedia.

Parry, M. and Wake, C. (eds) (1990) *Access and Alternative Futures for Higher Education*. London: Hodder & Stoughton.

Parsons, T. (1954) *Essays in Sociological Theory*. New York: The Free Press of Glencoe.

Pells, R. H. (1985) *The Liberal Mind in a Conservative Age: American Intellectuals in the 1940s and 1950s*. New York: Harper & Row.

Phillips, M. (1998) *All Must Have Prizes*. London: Warner Books.

Purdy, J. (1999) *For Common Things: Irony, Trust and Commitment in America Today*. New York: Alfred A. Knopf.

Rahe, P. (2003) 'The Idea of the Public Intellectual in the Age of the Enlightenment', in Melzer, Weinberger and Zinman (2003).

Revitch, D. (2003) *Language Police: How Pressure Groups Restrict What Students Learn*. New York: Alfred A. Knopf.

Robbins, B. (ed.) (1990) *Intellectuals, Aesthetics, Politics, Academics*. Minneapolis: University of Minnesota Press.

Robbins, B. (1993) *Secular Vocations: Intellectuals, Professionalism, Culture*. London: Verso.

Ross, A. (1989) *No Respect; Intellectuals and Popular Culture*. New York: Routledge.

Said, E. (1994) *Representations of the Intellectual*. London: Vintage.

Sennett, R. (2003) *Respect: The Formation of Character in an Age of Inequality*. New York: Norton.

Shils, E. (1972) *The Intellectuals and the Powers and Other Essays*. Chicago: University of Chicago Press.

Shorter Oxford English Dictionary, The (1965). Oxford: Clarendon Press.

Small, H. (ed.) (2002) *The Public Intellectual*. Oxford: Blackwell Publishing.

Spender, D. and Sarah, E. (1992) *Learning to Lose; Sexism and Education*. New York: Women's Press.

Stout, M. (2000) *The Feel-Good Curriculum; The Dumbing-Down of America's Kids in the Name of Self-Esteem*. Boston, MA: Perseus Books.

Strahern, M. (ed.) (2000) *Audit Cultures*. London: Routledge.

Tusa, J. (2003) *On Creativity; Interviews Exploring the Process*. London: Methuen.

Walden, G. (2001) *The New Elites: Making a Career in the Masses*. London: Penguin Books.

Wallinger, M. and Warnock, M. (eds) (2000) *Art for All? Their Policies and Our Culture*. London: Peer.

Young, M. (1961) *The Rise of the Meritocracy, 1870–2033: An Essay on Education and Equality*. Harmondsworth: Penguin Books.

Articles

Aronowitz, S. (2003) 'A Mills Revival?', *Logos* 2(3) (Summer 2003).

Berman, R. A. (1989) 'Perestroika for the University!', *Telos* 81 (Fall).

Bourdieu, P. (1989) 'The Corporatism of the Universal: The Role of Intellectuals in the Modern World', *Telos* 81 (Fall).

Brouwer, D. C. and Squires, C. R. (2003) 'Public Intellectuals, Public Life, And The University', *Argumentation and Advocacy* 39.

Gamson, W. A. (1999) 'Beyond the Science-versus-Advocacy Distinction', *Contemporary Sociology* 28(1).

Heinrich, K. (1989) 'The Spiritual Impoverishment of the German University', *Telos* 81 (Fall).

Karnoouh, C. (1989) 'Notes on the Crisis of the University', *Telos* 81 (Fall).

Luke, T. (1998) 'Miscast canons? The Future of Universities in an Era of Flexible Specialization', *Telos* 111 (Spring).

Pan, D. (1998) 'The Crisis of the Humanities and the End of the University', *Telos* 111 (Spring).

Piccone, P. (1989) 'The Reuniversalization of the University', *Telos* 81 (Fall).

Piccone, P. (1998) 'The End of Public Education?', *Telos* 111 (Spring).

Index